Managerial Attitudes and Performance

The Irwin-Dorsey Series in Behavioral Science

ARGYRIS *Interpersonal Competence and Organizational Effectiveness*

ARGYRIS *Organization and Innovation*

CARZO & YANOUZAS *Formal Organization: A Systems Approach*

GUEST *Organizational Change: The Effect of Successful Leadership*

KUHN *The Study of Society: A Unified Approach*

LAWRENCE & SEILER, WITH BAILEY, KATZ, ORTH, CLARK, BARNES, & TURNER *Organizational Behavior and Administration: Cases, Concepts, and Research Findings* Revised Edition

LYNTON & PAREEK *Training for Development*

MASLOW *Eupsychian Management: A Journal*

MASSARIK & RATOOSH *Mathematical Explorations in Behavioral Science*

ORTH, BAILEY, & WOLEK *Administering Research and Development: The Behavior of Scientists and Engineers in Organizations*

PORTER & LAWLER *Managerial Attitudes and Performance*

PRICE *Organizational Effectiveness: An Inventory of Propositions*

RUBENSTEIN & HABERSTROH (eds). *Some Theories of Organization* Revised Edition

SCOTT *The Management of Conflict*

SEILER *Systems Analysis in Organizational Behavior*

WHYTE *Men at Work*

WHYTE & HAMILTON *Action Research for Management*

Managerial Attitudes and Performance

LYMAN W. PORTER, Ph.D.

Professor and Associate Dean, Graduate School of
Administration
University of California, Irvine

EDWARD E. LAWLER, III, Ph.D.

Associate Professor of Administrative
Sciences and Psychology
Yale University

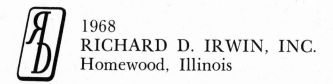

1968
RICHARD D. IRWIN, INC.
Homewood, Illinois

Preface

This book deals with a topic that is pertinent both to social scientists concerned with behavior in the work situation and to those individuals who occupy positions in the management of organizations. The topic concerns the relationships between the job attitudes of managers and their on-the-job performance.

We have approached this subject in two ways: first, by developing a conceptual model that attempts to specify some of the key variables—and their inter-relationships—that are involved in understanding the links between managers' attitudes and beliefs and their behavior in the work situation; second, by presenting relevant empirical data that were collected for the purpose of testing and elaborating the theoretical model. Thus, this is neither a strictly theoretical book nor a purely research book. Instead, it endeavors to bring to bear both realms to provide insights into this psychological and managerial problem.

Since Chapter 1 presents the rationale behind the development of the model and the nature of the study, we shall not repeat this information here. Rather, we wish to say a few words about our hopes concerning the ways in which this volume might prove useful to students and researchers, on the one hand, and those interested in direct organizational applications, on the other. For the former group, we see the model as providing a framework around which to organize some of the diverse literature relating to the motivation and satisfaction of employees, particularly those in management. We would also hope that both the model and the new research findings we report will stimulate some of our academic colleagues to undertake further, more refined studies in this area. For those who face day-to-day motivational situations in their work in organizational settings, we would like to feel that our model and findings have raised some relevant issues for them to consider, and that our final chapter has provided them with some leads about how to increase the usefulness of information gained from employee attitude assessments.

The attitude data that are analyzed in this book represent new research findings that have not been reported elsewhere, with the exception of certain sections of the chapter dealing with attitudes toward pay. These data on pay attitudes are based in part on E. E. L.'s thesis investigation and are related to two previous articles (Lawler, 1965a; Lawler, 1965b). Subsequent to the initial drafting of the manuscript for this book, we have presented portions of the theoretical model in two recent articles published in professional journals (Lawler & Porter, 1967a; Lawler & Porter, 1967b). In both of these articles, new and additional data have been reported that are relevant to the development and refinement of the model.

A field study such as this requires a high level of cooperation from officials in organizations that provided the managerial samples. Therefore, we are pleased to acknowledge the invaluable assistance of the following individuals who cleared various organizational paths for our data collection forays: Wilson Davis, E. E. Lawler, Jr., John E. Wilson, David Hess, Edgar Collings, John Swanson, Robert Hinman, Eric Neilson, James Cart, and Louis Simenson. That the efforts of these men resulted in superior performance can be attested to by the fact that our overall response rate for questionnaire returns averaged close to 90 percent.

Financial and administrative support of this project has been provided by the Institute of Industrial Relations and the Computer Center of the University of California, Berkeley, and by the Administrative Sciences Department of Yale University. Expert typing of the drafts of our manuscript has been handled by Mrs. Doris Bovee, Mrs. Elizabeth Poor, and Mrs. Sandra Walsh.

We are particularly indebted to two professional colleagues, David Kipnis and Victor Vroom, for their careful reading of the manuscript and their many helpful suggestions for changes and clarifications.

Finally, we are happy to acknowledge the support and encouragement of our wives, Meredith and Carol, and especially their willingness to put in extra hours on the home front while we put in long hours with the manuscript.

LYMAN W. PORTER

December, 1967   EDWARD E. LAWLER, III

Table of Contents

CHAPTER 1

Introduction

FOCUS OF THE BOOK

The relationship between attitudes and behavior has been a traditional topic of research for industrial psychologists as well as for psychologists working in many other fields. An interest in this issue prompted us to undertake the work that is reported in this book. In order to begin to understand this relationship, we found it necessary not only to collect a considerable amount of empirical data, but also to develop a theoretical model of the relationship between job attitudes and job performance. This model was designed both to help understand the data that would be generated in the present study and to provide a theoretical orientation that would stimulate future research.

For the purpose of our study, we decided to focus on only one broad class of attitudes and one broad class of behaviors—those that are job-related. It hardly seems necessary to elaborate on the importance of understanding human behavior that is job-related. Work has always been and continues to be the major nonfamily activity that is undertaken by most human beings. For most people, their work is more than just eight hours out of their waking life; it is a way of life that largely determines where they will live, with whom they will associate, and even what their children will become. Because of the centrality of work, it seems to be particularly appropriate that the study of the relationship between attitudes and performance focus on the work situation. Information gained from the work situation should be especially useful in understanding the attitude-behavior relationship elsewhere.

Attitudes traditionally have been studied by psychologists because they can provide important insights into human cognitive processes, and, ultimately, because they can contribute to the understanding and prediction of human behavior. In the present study we concentrated our attention upon a particular set of job attitudes because of our feeling that they are the most relevant ones for understanding employees' desires to perform effectively, the way in which employees carry out their work, and the kinds of rewards and satisfactions that are available from work. Job attitude research in industry typically has studied only one kind of attitude—the employee's satisfaction with his job. Such a focus follows what English and English (1958) call a narrowly limited definition of the term *attitude* that includes only approval and disapproval views. It is our contention that if attitude research is going to make significant contributions to the understanding of human behavior in work organizations, a broader conception is needed of what aspects of individual cognitive behavior are to be studied. The preferred definition of attitudes given by English and English (1958) — which includes all learned predispositions to react to an object or class of objects, as they are conceived to be—better fits our conception of the facets of cognitive behavior with which attitude research needs to be concerned. As Krech, Crutchfield, and Ballachey (1962) point out, attitudes include cognitive belief components, feeling components, and action tendency components. The data we have collected in the present study consist of verbal statements about objects that contain belief components as well as feeling components and action tendency components. Our own "attitude" is that both belief and evaluative cognitions need to be considered in order to understand job behavior. To look at either separately in relation to behavior makes it difficult to understand the tie-in between cognition and behavior.

The title of this book indicates that we plan to focus on one particular type of employee that can be found in all organizations —the manager. Obviously, this is a large and diverse group of people, but all have one thing in common. They are all held responsible for the job performance of persons other than themselves. The rapid expansion of our industrialized society has led to a situation in which the managerial role has achieved a level of importance that makes it a key job in today's world. The managerial job is becoming increasingly prevalent in our society and the manager finds himself in a position to influence complex enterprises that contain unparalleled human and physical resources. The pervasiveness, importance, and complexity of the managerial job demand that we learn as much as possible about it.

We also intend to concentrate our attention upon a particular aspect of managerial job behavior. Specifically, we are interested in that job behavior which determines how effectively a manager performs his job. Thus, our focus is upon the relationship between the attitudes of managers toward their jobs and the effectiveness of their performance in their jobs. In a very real sense, when one talks about human behavior in organizations, individual performance effectiveness is a *sine qua non*. It is the central issue for most organizations, and as a result provides a sort of magnified picture of the kind of attitude-behavior relationships that might be found if other types of behavior were being studied.

There is, of course, an important additional reason for studying managerial effectiveness. Increased knowledge in this area may lead to applications that will improve the effectiveness of organizations. There already exists a wealth of anecdotes and expressions of personal experience that purport to add to our understanding of what constitutes effective managerial behavior. However, with this kind of data it is difficult, if not impossible, to develop valid recommendations for effective managerial practice. Only by the scientific analysis of the preconditions for, and the consequences of, effective on-the-job behavior can we ever hope to arrive at practical recommendations that have some degree of merit and generality. In other words, careful research in the area must *precede* attempts to prescribe future courses of action. While it is not our main purpose in writing this book to develop such prescriptions, we will, nevertheless, discuss possible practical applications of our findings whenever we think the data warrant such considerations. (See especially Chapter 9.)

HISTORICAL PERSPECTIVE

Psychologists have been studying the interaction between work and workers for over half a century. Münsterberg's (1913) original textbook serves as a landmark, since it indicates the start of psychologists' concern with work behavior. However, the emphasis in this and other early work was not upon job attitudes nor upon managers' job behavior. Instead, psychologists focused upon techniques concerned with personnel selection and placement and upon problems of improving physical aspects of the work situation. Starting in the late 1930's, however, interest began to increase in the attitudes of employees and their relation to employee behavior. The strongest stimulant for this switch in emphasis was provided by the Hawthorne studies (Roethlisberger and Dickson, 1939). Later work by Lewin (Lewin, Lippit and White, 1939) and Coch and French (1948) served to emphasize the importance of individuals' attitudes and feelings about their work. By the late thirties and early forties it had become acceptable to study things like job satisfaction and the importance of work factors.

The study of workers' attitudes developed rapidly so that by the mid-fifties Herzberg *et al.* (1957) were able to find several hundred studies of workers' job attitudes. As Tannenbaum (1966) has pointed out, job attitudes are a distinctly psychological variable and, therefore, it is not too surprising that industrial psychologists have devoted so much attention to this topic. Herzberg *et al.* also found a number of studies, as did Brayfield and Crockett (1955), that focused upon the relationship between workers' job attitudes and their job behavior. Brayfield and Crockett, for example, cite more than 20 studies of the relationship between satisfaction and performance, while Herzberg *et al.* cite 26. These reviews also cite a number of studies of the relationship between satisfaction and employee turnover and absenteeism. Missing almost entirely from these reviews, however, were studies that look at managers' job attitudes. It is somewhat surprising that managers had not been studied, since they represent a highly significant and visible part of the work force of any organization. In addition, there are important reasons for believing that, since managers find themselves in a considerably different psychological environment from that of workers, the same kind of attitude-

behavior relationships that exist at the worker level may not necessarily hold at the managerial level. Likert (1961), for example,
has hypothesized that job satisfaction may be more closely related
to managerial performance than it is to worker performance.

The early 1960's mark the beginning of the large-scale studies
of managers' job attitudes. Studies by Rosen and Weaver (1960)
and Porter (1961) perhaps best signal the start of this trend. At
the present time, a clearly visible literature has developed on the
topic of managers' attitudes. Interestingly, this literature appears
to justify the conclusion that managers are indeed an identifiable
group whose attitudes are worth study in their own right, independent of the attitudes of workers. (For a review of this literature, see Porter and Lawler, 1965, and Vroom, 1965.) These
studies have focused on such topics as the relationship between
job satisfaction and management level, and job satisfaction and
organization size. Lacking until the present time, however, have
been studies of the relationship between managers' job attitudes
and their job behavior. For example, Vroom (1964), in reviewing
the literature on the relation between satisfaction and performance, found 20 studies that looked at this relationship; but only
three of these involved individuals with supervisory responsibilities, and even these looked only at the first-level supervisors.
Figure 1–1 illustrates our view of the current state of knowledge
of job attitudes. It shows that we know quite a bit about workers'
attitudes, somewhat less about the relationships between workers'
attitudes and performance, still less about managers' job attitudes,
and almost nothing about the relationship between managers'
job attitudes and job performance.

	JOB ATTITUDES IN GENERAL	JOB ATTITUDES IN RELATION TO PERFORMANCE
WORKERS		
MANAGERS		?

Figure 1–1. Characterization of Our Knowledge in the Area of Job
Attitudes.

A larger, and in some ways even more serious, gap exists when we shift from a consideration of studies of the relationship between attitudes and performance to a consideration of *theories* of the relationship between these two variables. With a few notable exceptions (e.g., Brayfield and Crockett, 1955; Georgopoulos, Mahoney, and Jones, 1957; Herzberg *et al.*, 1959; Triandis, 1959; Vroom, 1964), the amount of such theorizing has been thin in proportion to the magnitude of the issue. And especially of a *rara-avis* variety are studies that combine both empirical data and a theoretical orientation. Industrial psychologists have often been accused by their psychological peers of being the masters of atheoretical data collection or what has come to be known as "dust-bowl empiricism." One look at the literature on the relationship between attitudes and performance should be enough to convince anyone that this criticism has some merit.

It is our view that only with a testable theory available can any substantial progress be made in understanding the relationship between attitudes and performance. Past experience indicates that the atheoretical approach frequently produces at best a number of small isolated findings that do not fit together in any meaningful pattern, and thus, such findings provide little basis upon which to extrapolate to other situations. This, of course, has created a situation where particular findings in industrial psychology not only seldom suggest any significant implications for practice but, more importantly, they also are out of touch with advances being made in other areas of psychology.

Baxter (1965) has appropriately commented on this situation in his recent presidential address to the Division of Industrial Psychology of the American Psychological Association:

> We produce a seemingly endless stream of fragments leading to nowhere. We produce many new concepts without tying them to anything existing—largely because we lack something fundamental to which to tie them . . . . Theory is not an abstraction on the shelf but a daily tool, guiding us at all phases of our work, from conception of the problem to reporting the results. With this approach our research fragments will contribute to our conceptions and will "add up" to something meaningful.

In a comment that is perhaps even more directly relevant for this study, Guion and Gottier (1965) noted,

It must be admitted that industrial psychology lacks a general theory of work; it lacks a more specific theory of the relationship of motivational constructs to the behavior of an individual at his job; and it lacks even a substantial body of research explicitly aimed toward the development of such theories. In this vacuum, it is no wonder that raw empiricism is still an essential ingredient of practical personnel research. If the problem lies in the lack of relevance of existing theories, then the solution must surely lie in the design of research that will lead to a relevant theory.

MOTIVATION THEORY

It has been customary to study job attitudes concerned with satisfaction and need importance because of their assumed relationship to the employee's desire, willingness, or motivation to come to work and to perform his job. It is because the study of attitudes is so closely tied to the study of motivation and motivation theory that one can draw upon a considerable body of basic psychological theory to build a model of the relationship between job attitudes and job behavior. Indeed, any adequate theory of the relationship between attitudes and performance must contain within it a theory of motivation if it is to deal with attitudes concerning needs, values, and satisfactions. For these reasons we find it necessary at this point to review those aspects of motivation theory that appear to be particularly relevant to an understanding of the relationship between job attitudes and job performance. Furthermore, basic postulates and concepts from motivation theory form the basis upon which our own conceptual model of the relationship between attitudes and performance is based.

Motivation theory attempts to explain "how behavior gets started, is energized, is sustained, is directed, is stopped, and what kind of subjective reaction is present in the organism while all this is going on" (Jones, 1959). The obvious concern of motivation theory with the subjective reactions of the organism means that it must deal with attitude variables, and its emphasis on behavior opens up the entire question of the relationship between attitudes and behavior. Atkinson (1964) has argued that despite the fact that a great number of motivation theories have been proposed, there are only two basic theories that have been stated and developed to a comprehensive state. The first of these theories is the familiar "drive $\times$ habit" theory, and the other is "expectancy $\times$ value" theory.

Today's two dominant theories of motivation both have their philosophical roots in hedonism. The principles of hedonism can be traced directly back to the English utilitarians of the 18th and 19th centuries, most notably Jeremy Bentham and John Stuart Mill. According to the principles of hedonism, people are oriented away from pain and toward pleasure. A hedonistic calculus is theorized to operate in every situation so that people select from among alternatives on the basis of their assumptions about the relative amounts of pleasure and pain each has to offer. As an idea, hedonism has an obvious appeal because of its simplicity and because it appears to make good "common sense." However, as a psychological theory, it has proved to be untestable because of the problems involved in operationalizing its concepts. Most crucial, probably, is its failure to specify what kinds of experience are likely to be satisfying, and what kinds are likely to be dissatisfying.

Unless this is specified in advance, hedonism can deal with negative evidence by arguing that any particular event was either satisfying or dissatisfying, depending upon the behavior. Obviously, it is not long before a circular argument develops, with events or objects identified as satisfying solely because they are sought after. In short, hedonism lacks sufficient empirical content to be testable and fails to do a good job of either predicting or explaining behavior.

Drive Theory

"Drive" theory and "expectancy" theory essentially represent two different attempts to deal with the criticisms typically directed at hedonism. Drive theory is probably the best known of the two theories, and it has been and continues to be the dominant theory of motivation among experimental psychologists. One of the key starting points for this theory was Thorndike's (1911) statement of the "law of effect." According to the law of effect, responses which are accompanied or closely followed by satisfaction will be more likely to recur than those that are followed by discomfort. The law of effect has been called "hedonism of the past" because

it emphasizes previous behavior-reward connections. Present behavior is determined not by impending thoughts of pleasure but
by past associations. Thorndike attempted to avoid the argument
that his theory was circular by trying to operationalize his concept of satisfying and dissatisfying situations, but still he was
never completely able to answer this criticism.

The first important changes in, and extensions of, the law of
effect were made by Hull (1935). His version is perhaps the most
influential statement of drive theory. According to Hull (1943),
behavior is determined by the product of drive strength and habit
strength. Hull and many drive theorists were largely concerned
with physiological needs, and they thought of drive strength as
some function of the length of physiological deprivation. Habit
strength takes into account past learning and is concerned with
previous stimulus-response connections. Hull (1952) and Spence
(1956) have more recently updated drive theory in the light of
additional evidence, but it still contains the two basic elements
of habit strength and drive.

Expectancy Theory

The two most dominant figures in the original statement and
development of expectancy theory were Tolman (1932) and
Lewin (1938). Lewin's (1938) theory in particular is cognitive
in nature and, in contrast to the typical emphasis on animal behavior in drive theory, focuses more on human behavior. Basic to
both these theories is the conception that people have behavior
response "expectations" or "anticipations" about future events.
Presumably, these take the form of beliefs concerning the likelihood that a particular act will be followed by a particular outcome. Such beliefs or expectancies can take values between 0 (no
chance) and 1 (completely sure it will follow). This is obviously
a cognitive concept, since it refers to subjective rather than to
objective probabilities. This same concept has been referred to as
subjective probability by others (e.g., Edwards, 1954; Davidson,
Suppes, and Siegel, 1957). Expectancy theorists also assume that
people have preferences among outcomes, a la hedonism, although
they are less clear about stating why some outcomes are negatively
regarded and others are positively regarded. Expectancy theorists,

however, do seem to emphasize psychological motives more than do the drive theorists, who stress physiological motives. The terms reinforcement value, reward value, utility, and demand for goal have also been used to describe the concept that people have preferences among outcomes.

The decision that now remains to be made for our purposes concerns which theory we will adopt to serve as a framework upon which to build a model of the relationship between job attitudes and job performance. This decision is not one that involves choosing between basically different approaches to motivation, because there is a strong similarity between drive and expectancy theory. Rather, it is a decision that involves trying to determine which of two similar approaches to motivation is most compatible with our thinking about the relationship between job attitudes and job performance.

Drive and expectancy theory both contain the concept of an association between events. For drive theory this is called habit strength; for expectancy theory, an expectancy. Drive and expectancy theory also both contain an element of hedonism, since they talk about reinforcers on the one hand and valences on the other. In addition, both theories see the two basic elements combining in a multiplicative fashion, so that both theories indicate that in order for motivation to exist, there must be both positive outcomes and some kind of appropriate connection between behavior and the outcomes.

Differences between the Theories

There are perhaps three rather subtle differences between the two theories that should be noted. Atkinson (1964) has stressed the fact that there is a difference between the theories with respect to what is activated by the anticipation of the positively valent outcomes in the case of expectancy theory, and by drive in the case of drive theory. Expectancy theory argues that the anticipation of the positively valent outcome functions selectively on actions which are expected to lead to it. Drive theory views the magnitude of goal as a source of general excitement—a nonselective influence on performance. An example given by Atkinson illustrates this point.

Suppose a young male college student is working on his final examination in a course when the odor of perfume from an attractive girl in the seat behind him begins to tickle his nostrils and produce, ever so slightly, the arousal of the kind of anticipatory consummatory reaction we might imagine appropriate under these circumstances. If this slight anticipatory sexual arousal is all that happens, and the stimulus does not become so strong that a head-turning habit is also elicited, the young man should begin to work more vigorously at his examination according to the theory which says anticipatory goal reactions produce non-specific excitement; but there should be no change in the level of his performance (working on the examination) if the Expectancy $\times$ Value conception is correct. That is the moot point under discussion. (Atkinson, 1964, p. 281)

The two other differences between the theories also involve subtle points. The drive theory concept of habit strength emphasizes past stimulus-response connections, and thus weights past learning heavily. Expectancy theory, on the other hand, emphasizes the anticipation of response-outcome connections and thus places a greater emphasis upon anticipation of the future than upon past learning. Indeed it has been called "hedonism of the future."

The final distinction between the two theories centers upon how rewards or outcomes acquire their positive and negative qualities. For drive theory, this has traditionally come about through their ability to reduce the tension associated with the deprivation of certain physiologically based drives. It also states that some outcomes acquire their rewarding or aversive properties through their association with primary reinforcers. Outcomes that gain their values this way are typically referred to as secondary reinforcers. Expectancy theory has been much less explicit on this point. However, expectancy theorists seem typically to have included more than just physiological factors as determinants of valence. For example, needs for esteem, recognition, and self-actualization have been talked about by expectancy theorists as determinants of valence. This has undoubtedly come about because of the concern of expectancy theory with explaining performance. Drive theory, on the other hand, has focused largely on learning rather than performance and has not found it as necessary to deal with motives like self-actualization in order to explain this learning.

Despite these differences between the theories, it is still apparent that they contain similar basic elements. Thus, it appears that in almost every situation they will produce identical predictions (Atkinson, 1964). Not surprisingly, there seems to be no existing evidence that clearly supports the rejection of one theory and the acceptance of the other. The existing evidence thus can be used in support of either theory.

Preference for Expectancy Theory

Either theory could undoubtedly be used as a basis upon which to construct our model of the relationship between job attitudes and job performance, without any major differences appearing between the kinds of predictions, evidence interpretations, and recommendations for practice that would be developed on the basis of the model. Our preference, however, is to use expectancy theory as a basis upon which to establish our model. Like Vroom (1965), we find expectancy theory to be the best framework within which to approach the issue of managerial motivation. The work of a number of recent writers, most notably Atkinson (1964), Edwards (1954), Peak (1955), and Vroom (1964), has contributed significantly to the development of expectancy theory. The model which will be stated in the next chapter obviously draws upon the theorizing of these and other psychologists. Also, an article which particularly stimulated our own thinking, and which adopts an expectancy approach to motivation as well as presenting some data relevant to it, is "A Path-Goal Approach to Productivity" by Georgopoulos, Mahoney, and Jones (1957).

We decided to use an expectancy framework for our model for several reasons. Basically, the terminology and concepts involved seem to us to be more applicable to consideration of the complexities of human motivation and behavior and, therefore, more applicable to understanding the attitudes and performance of managers in organizations. The emphasis in expectancy theory on rationality and expectations seems to us to describe best the kinds of cognitions that influence managerial performance. We assume that managers operate on the basis of some sort of expectancies which, although based upon previous experience, are forward-oriented in a way that does not seem to be as easily handled by the concept of habit strength. The habit-strength concept seems to convey a rather narrow determinism of past experience in similar stimulus situations that for us is too mechanistic to account for the large individual differences and broad class of factors that appear to influence managers' behavior-outcomes associations.

Expectancy theory also greatly facilitates the incorporation of motives like status, achievement, and power into a theory of attitudes and performance. There is a considerable amount of evidence that the central motives for most managers are those for *achievement, self-actualization, power and status,* and *income and advancement.* For example, in comparison with nonmanagers, managers score higher on projective measures of achievement motivation (Veroff, Atkinson, Feld, and Gurin, 1960). Porter (1963) has found that managers rate as most important the need for self-actualization. Lawler (1966–a) has pointed out that income is very important to managers because of the breadth of the needs that it satisfies. In short, it appears that managerial motivation is based upon needs and motives that are not physiologically based in the same sense as are hunger and thirst. Because of this, and the emphasis of expectancy theory on explaining performance rather than learning, we find expectancy theory fits better into our attempt to understand managerial behavior.

Any model that uses expectancy theory as a starting point must deal with two major criticisms of this approach. First, these theories are criticized as being ahistorical because of their vagueness about the kind of previous learning experiences that produce different expectancies. We will attempt to deal with this in our model by indicating the way in which previous response-outcome associations and other factors influence an individual's expectancies. The second criticism that is often made of expectancy theory is that it does not specify how outcomes acquire positive or negative qualities for individuals. It is our hope that by focusing on outcomes that, like pay, are associated with the satisfaction of the important needs of managers, we can deal with this problem. Obviously, in order to answer the criticisms of expectancy theory, we are admittedly drawing upon aspects of drive theory, and we see this as desirable. In a sense, although we are going to use the language of cognitively oriented expectancy theorists, we are attempting to focus on the basic elements of motivation theory upon which there is fairly substantial agreement.

SUMMARY

So far we have emphasized the point that the study of the relationship between job attitudes and job performance is important because it can make contributions both to a motivational theory of work behavior and to organizational practices designed to increase performance effectiveness. At the present time, relatively little is known about the relationship between job attitudes and job behavior. Particularly lacking are (1) data on the relationship between *managers'* job attitudes and their job behavior, and (2) a conceptual model of the attitudes-performance relationship. Our book is designed to try to meet these two needs.

Chapter 2 will present our conceptual model of the relationship between job attitudes and job performance. The model has its roots in the expectancy theories of motivation and attempts to specify the kinds of job attitudes that should be related to job performance. In addition, it specifies which attitudes should precede and, therefore, cause performance; and which should be dependent upon performance. The next chapter explains the methodology of our empirical study and the characteristics of the data that we collected in order to begin to test the model. Chapters 4–7 present the empirical data relevant to the model. The reader will note that the order of these chapters is dictated by the model, since chapters 4 and 5 deal with attitudes that we see as largely antecedent to performance, whereas chapters 6 and 7 deal with attitudes which the model specifies are largely dependent upon performance. In Chapter 8 we attempt to reevaluate the model in the light of our data. Finally, in Chapter 9 we propose some implications for practice that seem to arise from the model and the data.

CHAPTER 2

The Theoretical Model

The previous chapter described the origins of this study and briefly noted some of the relevant literature. As mentioned earlier, in designing a study to investigate the relationship of managerial attitudes to managerial performance, we found it necessary to develop a conceptual scheme to guide our thinking. The result is a model, outlined in this chapter, that attempts to relate effort, performance, satisfaction, and other key variables. The model is, therefore, presented as a mechanism to integrate the findings from our investigation. More importantly, however, it is presented with the hope of encouraging additional research to test various implications that follow from it. No claims are made that this model provides for a total explanation of the relationships existing between job attitudes and job performance. Future research may indicate that other important variables should be included in the model. Our intent in this respect has been a minimal one: to indicate at least some of the important variables and the hypothesized relationships that exist between and among them.

One feature of the model is that it leads to some clearly testable hypotheses. However, from our point of view, its most important feature is that it provides a way of thinking about the relationships among a large number of variables that have not previously been combined in a meaningful manner. Later research may well uncover evidence that some of the particular relationships do not exist in the manner predicted by the model. If parts of the model, therefore, lend themselves to specific disproof and, consequently, to specific improvement as a means of explanation, then its development will have served a useful purpose. Regardless of this possibility, however, the major concern in the present study is to see whether the model provides a reasonably coherent framework for understanding the total pattern of findings emerging from the obtained data.

In the first of the remaining two parts of this chapter each of the nine separate variables in the model, as shown in Exhibit A, will be defined and discussed. Following this description of the nine variables will be a discussion of the relationships that are hypothesized to exist among them.

VARIABLES CONTAINED IN THE MODEL

Value of Reward

This variable refers to the attractiveness of possible outcomes to individuals. The focus in our model and the emphasis in our discussion will be on positively valued outcomes, i.e., rewards.[1] Various rewards that a person might hope to obtain—e.g., the friendship of fellow workers, a promotion, a merit salary increase, an intrinsic feeling of accomplishment—are differentially desired by a given individual. Likewise, a given potential reward is differentially desired by different individuals. For example, the friendship of peers (i.e., workers at the same job level) might be highly desired by a young girl recently graduated from high school who does not plan to remain in the work force for more than a few years. This reward would have, then, a high positive value for her. On the other hand, a promotion might have very little posi-

---

[1] Although, as Vroom (1964) has noted, some possible outcomes have aversive qualities that result in their having negative values, our model will focus on positively valued outcomes. This is because the data we have collected in the present investigation are specifically limited to measuring the degree to which a particular positive outcome (pay) is found to be desirable. We should point out, however, that the model can just as well substitute "value of outcomes" (both desirable and aversive), for "value of rewards," with no major effects on other variables in the model or on predictions from it.

EXHIBIT A
The Theoretical Model

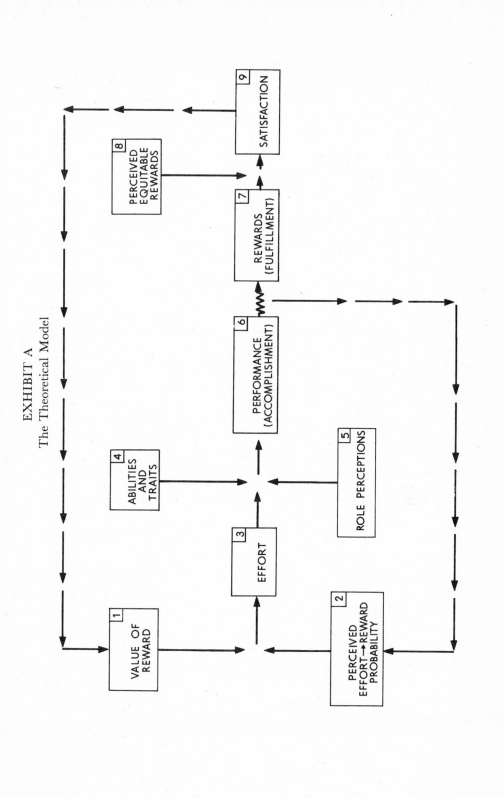

tive value for her because she does not want to take on increased responsibilities. This situation could be exactly reversed for a middle manager in a large corporation. While he does not desire to be on unfriendly terms with his peers, this potential reward (of peer friendship) might be not particularly important to him in the job situation because he has so many friendships in his out-side-the-organization and off-the-job contacts. A promotion, though, might be a reward of extremely high value to such a person.

It should be noted that the model does not specify in detail how various rewards acquire differential value. As will be discussed later in this chapter, the model does contain a feedback loop from "satisfaction" to "value of reward." The reason for the feedback loop is to indicate that we are making the assumption that one of the ways that potential rewards acquire value is through their ability to satisfy various fundamental needs (e.g., security needs, self-actualization needs, etc.). Beyond this hypothesized impact of satisfaction, however, the model does not further specify the process of value acquisition by rewards. The model merely posits that for any individual at a particular point in time there are a variety of potential rewards to which he attaches differential value.

To measure the value of a reward or rewards to an individual, several methods are possible (see Vroom, 1964). Chief among these are to ask a person: (1) to make an actual choice among two or more alternatives in a situation in which he anticipates that the attainment of these outcomes will be affected by his behavior; (2) to rank or rate, on an attitude scaling device, the value of different rewards to himself; or (3) to complete some sort of projective device such as the TAT or a sentence completion test from which some other person (i.e., the tester) infers the values of different rewards for the individual under consideration. The second of these three approaches tends to be the most feasible in field research situations and therefore has been used somewhat more widely than the other two methods.

To summarize, *value of reward* refers to how attractive or desirable is a potential outcome of an individual's behavior in the work situation.

Effort–Reward Probability

This variable refers to an individual's expectations concerning the likelihood that given amounts of rewards depend upon given amounts of effort on his part. Such an expectation can in turn be divided into two subsidiary expectations:

1. The probability that *reward* depends upon *performance*.
2. The probability that *performance* depends upon *effort*.

Frequently, theoretical presentations that invoke the concept of probability or expectancy of reward in explaining job performance fail to note the fact that these two distinct components are involved. We hypothesize that the two subsidiary probabilities are related in an interactive way such that if either is low, the probability that *reward* depends upon *effort* must necessarily also be low. Let us try to make these points clear by an example:

Suppose that a manager highly desires a transfer to the salubrious climate of the West Coast (such a transfer having a high *value,* in our terms). The manager might feel that his chances of obtaining the transfer have very little to do with his level of performance, either because virtually no transfers are being made and no amount of performance will help, or because transfers are being made but they depend on factors other than performance (random selection, personal whims of the boss, etc.). In any event, if he feels that his chances of a transfer do not depend upon his performance, then presumably he should also feel that they do not depend upon the amount of effort he puts into his job, and therefore he would perceive a low effort-reward probability. However, *even if* he feels that receiving a transfer does depend on performance, he may not feel that performance is related to effort. The reason for this would be a belief that, although the organization will definitely give a transfer for a certain level of performance, he himself is not capable of achieving that performance even with a high level of effort. In other words, he might be thinking something like: "I know if I sold x amount of our products the company would transfer me, but it would be practically impossible for me to sell that much, no matter how hard I tried."

A further complication that could arise would be a situation in which the manager feels that effort will result in rewards even though it does not necessarily result in performance. In this case, the organization would be perceived by the manager as paying off for "trying hard" but not necessarily for actual accomplishments. If this were the situation, the perceived probability that effort can lead to a certain level of performance would not influence the amount of effort the manager would put forth on his job. Here, the prediction would be that the manager would exert effort (because "exerting effort" is rewarded), but such effort might be diffuse rather than highly productive.

An important point to mention in connection with this variable (effort-reward probability) is that we are defining probability in terms of *perceived* probability on the part of the particular individual whose performance and satisfaction we are trying to explain. Thus, in the above example, the actual probability of a manager obtaining a transfer as the direct result of his efforts might be high (i.e., his superiors have definite plans to transfer him if his performance reaches a certain level, and he is capable of that level with a reasonable amount of effort), but the perceived probability might be quite low because the manager thinks that his efforts will in no way affect his chances. His behavior, in terms of what he will try to do, will be determined by his own expectation—his perceived expectation, in other words, whether or not this is in accord with the "real facts" of the situation. (Simon's concept of "bounded rationality" is relevant to the relationship between the individual's perceptions and the objective situation. For a brief discussion of this concept see Taylor's 1965 commentary.)

Measurement of this variable—effort-reward probability—as we have defined it, ordinarily would require obtaining statements of expectancies from the individuals whose behavior is being studied. Such statements could be directed to the reward-effort relationship; however, two expectancies could be obtained—one concerning the reward-performance relationship and the other the performance-effort relationship. If the latter approach were used, the two expectancies would be combined (probably multiplicatively) to obtain the perceived probability that reward depends upon effort. Regardless of whether a single probability or two probabilities are being obtained, it is important to try to minimize factors in the measurement situation that would cause respondents to give answers that they themselves recognize do not honestly represent their opinions. In addition to obtaining perceived probabilities from the subjects themselves in a study, it is always possible to try to obtain data on the actual relationship between effort and rewards (e.g., superiors' ratings of effort put forth by subordinates could be correlated with the pay given to these subordinates). Such information would not supplant the subjective probabilities, but would add supplementary facts that could be useful in understanding the subjects' perceptions of the probabilities.

In summary, *effort-reward probability* refers to an individual's perceptions of whether differential rewards are based on differential amounts of effort on his part in the work situation.

Effort

By effort, we mean the amount of energy an individual expends in a given situation. In nontechnical terms, "How hard is the person trying?" Of course, by energy we do not mean simply muscular movement. In many jobs, especially in management, this would refer to mental or intellectual effort—the extent to which an individual concentrates on a given activity in the application of his thinking.

Effort is a key variable in our model. As such, it must clearly be distinguished from another variable, performance. If we were referring to a baseball game, *effort* would correspond to the exertion made by a shortstop to try to stop a ground ball and throw the runner out, whereas *performance* would refer to whether or not the out was actually made. Although the two variables frequently are highly positively correlated—i.e., high effort often goes with good performance—this is not a necessary situation. College professors frequently encounter students who claim (probably quite truthfully in most cases) that they put in long hours and great concentration in studying for an exam—thus their effort was high; yet their performance, or score, was low.

We will explain in more detail later in the chapter why effort occupies such an important place in the model. For the moment, let us merely make the point that it is our view that what is commonly called "motivation" (the combination of the value of rewards and the perceived probability that reward depends on effort) should be more highly related to measures of effort than to measures of performance. In other words, the effects of motivation should show up more directly in the degree of effort expended, rather than in performance results.

A number of different means can be employed to measure effort. For this variable we can use self-reports, the reports of others, and (in certain very limited types of job situations) physical measurements. In obtaining either self-reports or reports from others we not only can ask about effort directly (e.g., for a supervisor, "rank your subordinates on the amount of effort they put into their jobs"), but we also can ask about other behaviors that should give indirect indications of effort. For example, a manager (or his superior) might be asked how many times he has come in early to the job over a given length of time, or how many evenings a week he spends in job-related activities. Or, in the case of a salesman, we can obtain the number of calls he makes on prospects. When obtaining these indirect measures, we should also be obtaining information on their relevancy for measuring effort. It is possible, for example, for an individual to come in early, work late and still not expend very much effort (mental or physical energy) in carrying out his job. The point is, there are a variety of possible measures of effort and, unlike the two previous variables, these measures are not restricted chiefly to self-reports. Observers frequently may be in a good position to judge effort, since this is a variable that, to a large extent, is externally expressive.

To summarize, *effort* refers to the energy expended to perform some task, but does not necessarily correlate with how successfully the task is carried out.

Abilities and Traits

This set of variables refers to relatively stable, long-term individual characteristics—e.g., personality traits, intelligence, manual skills, etc.—that represent the individual's currently developed power to perform. In our model, such abilities and traits are to be considered as relatively independent of immediate situational factors. This is not to say that abilities cannot be expanded by training or that personality traits cannot be influenced by psychotherapy; it is to say, rather, that abilities and traits are assumed not to fluctuate widely over short periods of time. In this sense, then, they are relatively long-term and not easily changed characteristics of the individual.

As will be explained later, *abilities and traits* are hypothesized to interact with *effort* and with *role perceptions* to determine *performance*. They put a current upper limit on the performance resulting from applications of effort. (If additional training resulted in improved abilities, for example, then a new upper limit would be placed on performance possibilities.) A person who has no musical abilities will never be a great pianist, no matter how much effort and practice he puts into the task of mastering this musical instrument. Likewise, a manager who has relatively low intellectual power or capacity (i.e., a low IQ) will be quite unlikely to be able to deal effectively with decisions that require highly abstract thought processes. This is not to say that a person with limited ability in a given area (e.g., intelligence) cannot compensate a great deal for his lack of broad capacity; however, it does imply that given two individuals who put forth equivalent effort in a given area of endeavor, the one possessing a greater amount of the relevant trait or ability will accomplish more—he will achieve a higher level of performance.

Measures of traits and abilities are provided by common psychometric devices. For example, intelligence can be measured by the Stanford-Binet, the Wechsler-Bellevue Intelligence Scale, or other similar measures. Manual dexterity can be measured by the Purdue Pegboard or the Minnesota Rate of Manipulation Test. In the personality areas, the California Psychological Inventory, the Minnesota Multiphasic Personality Inventory, the Edwards Personal Preference Scale, etc., can be used to measure specific traits. Obviously none of these measures is perfect, in the sense that for a specific individual they can misjudge the limits of actual performance which this person currently is capable of achieving. Given a group of individuals, however, the more soundly developed instruments can provide a reasonably accurate ranking of relative abilities and capacities.

To summarize, in considering performance we must take into

account the relatively long-term characteristics of individuals that remain largely unaffected by momentary changes in their environmental situation, namely their *abilities and traits.*

Role Perceptions

This variable refers to the *direction* of effort—the kinds of activities and behaviors the individual believes he *should* engage in to perform his job successfully. If his perceptions of his role correspond to those of his superiors in his organization, then he will be applying his effort where it will count the most for successful performance as defined by the organization. If his perceptions are "incorrect" (i.e., do not correspond to those of his superiors), then it is possible that he may expend a great deal of effort without organizationally defined successful performance taking place.

Let us take a couple of examples to illustrate what we mean by role perceptions in our model. If we were considering an academic situation, we might think of a case where a student puts in a great deal of effort studying his reading assignments but very little effort in studying his notes taken in lectures. If the exam is based largely on questions taken from lecture material, then his performance will presumably not be very high even though his total effort was great. If, on the other hand, he had spent considerable effort on studying his lecture notes, then presumably his performance on the exam would be better than that of another student of similar intellectual ability who had put in relatively less effort in a review of the lecture notes.

Shifting to an example from the business world, we might consider a lower-echelon supervisor who believes that the best way to perform well on his job (in order to gain the reward of promotion) is to become highly knowledgeable in his technical specialty, such as chemical engineering. If his superiors considered technical proficiency to be a highly important qualification for advancement, then his efforts to improve himself in this feature of his role should pay off. If, however, they consider broad administrative capabilities as a prime requisite for advancement, then the effort put into improving his technical knowledge of chemical engineering might actually be a detriment to successful role performance, since it took time away from his opportunities to improve his administrative proficiency.

Since role perceptions, as we define them, refer to *where* the individual thinks he can most profitably apply his efforts, they are best measured by some sort of report from the individual himself. Such reports can take the form of narrative descriptions of the role, or directive questionnaire items that ask the subject to rate or rank the traits and characteristics required for the job. The important thing is to obtain information on the individual's perceptions—preferably, information that is in some way quantifiable.

To summarize, *role perceptions* deal with the way in which the individual defines his job—the types of effort he believes are essential to effective job performance.

Performance

This variable refers to how much successful role achievement (behavior) is accomplished. It is the variable that industrial psychologists are talking about when they use the term "productivity." We have adopted the term "performance" rather than "productivity" in order to avoid the somewhat narrow connotations implied in the latter word when it is used to describe physical output from an employee. As we discussed previously, performance is the end result of the application of effort. It is that aspect of an employee's behavior which organizations are most desirous of measuring and influencing.

Job performance, as we are using the term, is made up of a broad range of more specific behaviors. However, it must be kept clearly in mind that we are using this term only in reference to types of behavior associated with organizationally relevant tasks. Performance does not mean the same thing as behavior in general. Let us illustrate. A given employee may smoke a great deal each day while at work for the organization. Smoking, in this instance, would be part of the employee's behavior, but not part of his performance. This same employee, also while at work, may maintain very friendly relations with his fellow employees. Such behavior may or may not be considered part of his job performance, depending upon the nature of his job. If his job requires a great deal of interaction with other employees, then the maintenance of good (or poor, as the case may be) relations with these individuals would be considered an aspect of his job performance. On the other hand, if his job—as defined by the organization—does not require much interaction with other employees, then his maintenance of friendly relations would be considered an aspect of his behavior but not of his job performance. Finally, if this same employee makes extremely valuable contributions to group meetings called to discuss organizational problems, then such behavior is clearly a part of his performance.

From the point of view of the organization, an employee, especially if he is a manager, can contribute to the organization's goals in a variety of ways. Consequently, a company or firm has many potential aspects of a person's behavior it can consider in evaluating his performance. The problem for the organization is to choose which particular aspects to measure, and how to measure them. Basically, three types of measures are possible, with only the first two types being commonly used by most companies.

One type of measure of performance involves objective, verifiable indices. Depending on the type of job a person has, such measures might include rate of output from a machine a person is operating, amount of sales over a given period of time, the production of a group of employees reporting to a manager, and so forth. This type of measure has all of the advantages associated with quantification. It has the danger that the objective measure may be the result of factors other than the individual's efforts. For example, one salesman may make higher sales than another, not because he tries harder or is in fact a better salesman, but rather because his sales territory is superior. Also, it is important to keep in mind that certain aspects of performance that might be quite quantifiable may not be very important in the long run to the organization. The number of letters a typist turns out in a day may not be as important as the quality of these letters (which is a much less quantifiable aspect of behavior) and the typist's ability to correct poor grammar.

A second type of measure of performance involves ratings of individuals by someone other than the person whose performance is being considered. Most commonly, of course, this takes the form of a boss rating or ranking his subordinates. Such ratings may be on an informal basis—a boss tells his own superiors that Smith is better than Jones; or it may be on a quite formal basis where the ratings are written down with elaborate commentaries and explanations. Also, ratings may be on a global, overall basis, where the rater tries to consider all relevant aspects of an individual's performance and then gives him a summary rating; or they may be on a basis where specific aspects or characteristics of performance are considered. In any event, the rating or ratings that emerge are subjective evaluations. The fact that they are subjective, however, does not necessarily mean they are inferior to objective measures of performance. As pointed out above, objective measures *may* be of aspects of performance that are not very crucial to the organization, whereas ratings *may* take into account less tangible aspects of performance that are quite important to the success of the organization. Such ratings as we are talking about here may be made by immediate superiors, higher-level superiors, peers, subordinates, or anyone else who comes into contact with the person being rated and has some sort of opportunity to observe his performance in the tasks that comprise his job.

Self-appraisal and self-ratings constitute the third type of performance measures. In the past, this type has been used only infrequently by companies in their day-to-day operations. However, in the future it is likely that firms will pay somewhat more attention to this kind of evaluation of performance. The reason for this probable shift is that self-ratings are compatible with, in fact a major part of, current trends in performance appraisal whereby the subordinate is encouraged to take an active role in setting his own goals and then measuring his progress toward these goals. Thus, while self-ratings typically may not be made on as formal a basis as are supervisory ratings, there is in the future likely to be greater encouragement by organizations for the individual manager to evaluate his own performance. In any event, regardless of how much the organization itself utilizes this method of performance evaluation in practice, the method can still serve as a useful measure for the researcher interested in relationships between performance and other variables. As in the case with supervisory ratings, self-ratings are purely subjective and cannot be "validated" in any meaningful way. If a given manager rates himself high on a given aspect of performance, even though others rate him quite low, his self-rating still may be a truthful (and in this sense "valid") expression of his opinion.

To summarize, *performance* refers to a person's accomplishment on tasks that comprise his job. Performance, in essence, is the net effect of a person's effort as modified by his abilities and traits and by his role perceptions. It can be evaluated by objective measures such as physical output, or by subjective measures such as ratings made by others or ratings made by the individual himself.

Rewards

This term refers to desirable outcomes or returns to a person that are provided by himself or by others. Two features of this definition should be stressed. First, the outcomes or returns must be positively valued by the individual. If he receives something that he does not want, this would not be considered a reward. Second, such outcomes can be either intrinsic to the person's own behavior, such as a feeling of accomplishment, or extrinsic in the sense that other people provide them, as when the company increases a manager's pay on the basis of the recommendation of a superior.

How do we measure the amount of rewards that individuals receive from their jobs? For intrinsic rewards, the only way is to ask the person concerning his feelings. By definition, only he knows whether he has rewarded himself intrinsically. For extrinsic rewards, one obvious way is to look at objective company actions. For a given individual, such measures as the current pay or salary, the number and size of salary increases, the number of promotions per unit of time, and so forth, could provide relevant information on the rewards a person has received. However, there are great dangers in using objective records as a measure of rewards obtained from job performance. First, what the company regards as a reward (e.g., a promotion) may not be regarded as such by the individual recipient. Hence, for him, it is not a reward. Second, the mere information that somebody has received a given reward (even granting that the person himself also feels it is a reward) provides no data on the degree of connection the individual sees between his performance and the reward. For these reasons, it is desirable to supplement objective information by questioning the individual himself. He is the best judge of whether or not he has received rewards, how large they are (to him), and the degree of their perceived connection to performance.

To summarize, *rewards* are desirable states of affairs that a person receives from either his own thinking or the action of others. For predicting future performance, the most important things to know about rewards are their perceived size and their perceived degree of connection to past performance.

Perceived Equitable Rewards

This variable refers to the level or amount of rewards that an individual feels he *should* receive as the result of a given level of performance. It can also refer to the amount of rewards an individual feels should be attached to a particular position or job in the organization. (In this latter case it is a concept of equity associated with the job, whereas in the former case it is a concept of equity associated more personally with the individual's own particular accomplishments in that job.)

In any job most individuals have an implicit notion (which they frequently are willing to state explicitly) concerning the amount of rewards that ought to be available for a person performing the type of work required in that job. Such notions would be based on the individual's perception of the requirements for a person to be able to fill the position, the demands that the tasks make on the individual, the contributions that the individual makes to the organization in that job, and so forth. Frequently, of course, the individual will take into account factors that the organization (or boss) might not consider at all in deciding the equitable or fair amount of rewards that the organization should provide.

Again, as with some of the previous variables discussed in our model, measurement of this variable depends primarily upon obtaining an expression from the individual involved as to what he considers a fair or appropriate level of reward. Such judgments could be made for the person by other individuals, but the inference that these necessarily would be accurate representations of

the feelings of the person in question usually would not be justified.

To summarize, *perceived equitable rewards* are defined as the
amount of rewards that a person feels is fair, given his performance
on the tasks he has been asked to undertake by the organization.

Satisfaction

This is a derivative variable. It is defined as the extent to which
the rewards actually received meet or exceed the perceived equitable level of rewards. To the degree that equitable rewards exceed
actual rewards, the person is dissatisfied. Thus, a small difference
of this kind would indicate relatively great satisfaction (i.e., little
dissatisfaction), and a large difference would indicate relatively
low satisfaction (i.e., great dissatisfaction).

The important feature of this definition of satisfaction is that
satisfaction is only in part determined by the level of rewards
actually received. In addition to knowing about rewards actually
received, we must also know what the person expected in terms
of equitable rewards in order to gauge his degree of satisfaction.
A simple example suffices. Two students turn in papers. One gets
a grade of B, the other a grade of C. If satisfaction were synon-
ymous with rewards received, the first student should be more
satisfied with his grade. However, if the first student felt his
paper deserved an A and he received "only" a B, we would consider him to be (and act) more dissatisfied than the student who
expected a C and received a C. Likewise in a business context, it
is quite easy for a man who receives an increase of $50 a month in
his salary to be more dissatisfied (i.e., less satisfied) than a man
who receives a $25 raise, if the first man's expectation of the
amount of increase that ought to have been given him far exceeded his actual increase, while the second man's views of an
appropriate increase were close to what he received.

It is, of course, true that if, for a given group of people, the
expectations of individuals about what they should receive in the
way of rewards are about equal from one person to another, their
satisfaction will be determined by the rewards they actually receive. (In this case, the amount of rewards felt to be equitable
acts like a constant number and could be ignored.) However, if

there are variations in feelings of what is appropriate among a group of people, then satisfaction may or may not correlate positively with the amount of rewards received.

Measurement of satisfaction obviously involves measurement of the two elements that define it: the perceived or expected equitable level of rewards, and the level of rewards seen as actually received. The ways of measuring each of these two variables have already been discussed in the preceding subsections of this chapter. In order to compute satisfaction, the amount of rewards received is subtracted from the amount felt to be equitable.

To summarize, *satisfaction* is defined as the extent to which rewards actually received meet or exceed the perceived equitable level of rewards. The greater failure of actual rewards to meet or exceed perceived equitable rewards, the more dissatisfied a person is considered to be in a given situation.

RELATIONSHIPS BETWEEN AND AMONG VARIABLES

So far in this chapter we have discussed separately each of the nine variables in the model. In the remaining part of the chapter we shall consider the interrelationships among the variables that are crucial for the theory. Historically speaking, the relationship receiving the most attention has been that between performance and satisfaction. However, we shall first consider how the value of rewards and perceived effort-reward probabilities combine to create effort, and how effort leads to performance. At the end, we shall consider two feedback relationships: the effects of rewards on perceived effort-reward probabilities, and the effects of satisfaction on the value of a reward.

Value of Reward and Effort–Reward Probability

We hypothesize that these two variables interact together to produce performance: The greater the value of a reward and the higher the perceived probability that effort will lead to this reward, the greater the effort.

Although we do not specify, in our model, exactly *how* these two variables interact to produce effort, we incline towards the view that the interaction is almost certainly multiplicative rather than additive. We find it difficult to believe that if either variable were close to zero there would be very much effort put forth in the task situation. In other words (and stating the form of the interaction between these two variables in the most conservative way), each variable—value of reward and probability that reward depends on effort—is a necessary but not sufficient condition for effort to be put forth in a job.

Effort in Relation to Performance

The diagram of the model on page 17 indicates two features of the effort-performance relationship that we hypothesize to exist. First, we are stating that increased effort can be expected to lead to increased performance, at least under most conditions. We are aware that a few laboratory studies carried out both on animals and on humans have found performance decrements under intense levels of motivation. Hence, it is possible that at exceptionally high levels of effort, performance might actually be decreased. However, it must be pointed out that there is little or no evidence available concerning the effects of prolonged applications of ex- tremely high effort in the normal job situation. Except in emer- gencies, it is doubtful that very many individuals try to exert such excessive effort day in and day out in the performance of their jobs. Therefore, within the typical ranges of effort ordinarily possi- ble in most jobs, we would maintain that higher levels of effort will usually lead to higher performance.

Second, we are stating that the relationship between effort and performance must be qualified to include the effects of two other variables: abilities and traits, and role perceptions. Before dis- cussing their hypothesized effects, we should hasten to acknowl- edge that there are, obviously, many environmental factors that also intervene to influence the relationship of effort to perfor- mance. For example, equipment features often place limits on the amount of output that will result from effort by a production line worker, or particular sales territories may give certain salesmen advantages that result in extra output unrelated to extra effort. In any case, our model does not take into account such external environmental factors because they represent "spurious" factors in understanding the psychological and human determinants of performance. Clearly, however, they affect performance per se.

Since our model specifies abilities and role perceptions as the two major human-type variables that interact with effort to determine performance, let us consider the hypothesized action of each of them in influencing this effort-performance relationship.

With respect to abilities (including traits), we earlier defined this variable as the "currently developed power to perform" of the individual. This definition implies that there is a ceiling in current possible performance and also that abilities are involved in translating activity (mental or physical or both) into task performance. We hypothesize that the interaction of effort and ability is of a multiplicative nature. The evidence for this contention has been reviewed by Lawler (1966–a) and Vroom (1964), and although it is not extensive, we find it empirically, logically, and psychologically convincing.

Role perceptions enter into the relationship between effort and performance (holding abilities constant) by determining the direction of the application of effort. High effort, if misdirected, will not result in high *task-relevant* performance (as seen by the person evaluating the performance). Another way of saying this is that the accuracy of role perceptions determines the proportion of effort that is relevant to task performance. As with abilities, we assume the interaction of role perceptions with effort to be of a multiplicative nature.

Because both role perceptions and abilities are assumed to intervene between effort and performance, the model indicates that effort will not be perfectly related to performance. This point has important implications for the relationship that should exist between the two determinants of effort (value of reward and effort-reward probabilities) and performance. These two variables should be more closely related to effort than to performance.

Performance in Relation to Rewards

In the work situation a desired outcome usually *but not necessarily* has some relation to performance. In fact, the degree of connection that an individual sees between his performance and his rewards is a key part of our whole theoretical system. We hypothesize that the greater the connection, the more likely a person is to exert effort to obtain a high level of performance. Many times, however, such connections are quite nebulous or indirect. This imperfect connection is represented by a wavy line in the diagram of our model. The wavy line is meant to indicate that rewards may be, but do not necessarily have to be, linked to performance differences.

Let us consider several examples of performance-reward connections. The salary that a person receives after six months at work is a reward, in the sense of being a desired outcome (i.e., preferable to no salary). If a company always hires new college graduates at x hundred dollars per month, and automatically gives each such new junior executive a raise of $50 per month after six months, then the new salary (x + $50) is presumably more rewarding than the initial salary. However, the new man is quite unlikely to see a connection between his own specific behavior and the new rate. If, a year later, he and a number of others (but not all others) get another increase, then he is likely to see some connection because he perceives that his performance was good enough to keep up with most of his colleagues and was better than the minority who did not get a raise. Here, the connection between behavior and performance would be somewhat indirect but not entirely absent. If, after another year, this manager received a raise that he knew was 50 percent greater than the raise that anyone else with his seniority had received, the connection between performance and reward probably would be seen as quite direct. The person is likely to think something like: "I must have gotten a large increase because the company thought I had been doing a better job than most of my friends who joined at the same time I did."

It should be clear from the foregoing that organizations (and individual superiors) can choose to adopt one or more of a number of different policies with regard to how closely they want to tie rewards to performance. If they chose to reward randomly, then there probably would be no perceived connection. If they chose to reward a given group of employees across the board (e.g., 5 percent cost-of-living increases to everyone in the organization; five-year pins to anyone who has stayed with the organization for that length of time, regardless of performance; rotational job assignments to every new management hire after six months, etc.), then again there would be very little, if any, perceived connection between rewards and performance. If, on the other hand, pay increases or a challenging new job assignment were granted only when specific levels of performance had been achieved, then it is likely that most individuals receiving such rewards would regard them as being connected to performance. Such a reward policy would be one that we might term a "differential extrinsic reward" policy.

The provision of differential extrinsic rewards is a function of three factors: (1) The organization's ability to discriminate among individual differences in performance. The organization's ability is, in this respect, in turn usually a function of the superior's ability to discriminate differences in achievement. If the superior or some other agent of the organization is unable to make such discriminations, then it is obviously impossible for the organization to attach differentially desirable outcomes to differential performance. (2) The organization's capability to give rewards. Even though the organization may be able to make discriminations among differences in performance, it may not be able to provide rewards. For example, in a given situation it may be the consensus of superiors that among a given group of subordinate managers Black is superior to Miller in performance and deserves the next promotion. However, there may be no vacancies available at the next level in the organization, and hence Black cannot be promoted for some time. (And, by the time he is eventually promoted, this action may not be seen by Black as a result of performance at the previous time in question.) Of course, substitute rewards may be possible, and the simple communication of the consensus of the superiors to Black may be a reward (assuming he desires to know that his superiors think well of him even if this is not accompanied by a promotion). (3) The organization's willingness to give rewards. A superior may be able to discriminate differences in performance and may have various rewards available that he could provide to the better performers. However, for various reasons he may not choose to do so. He might be jealous of a subordinate's accomplishment and thus not want to encourage him to even greater performance, and so he withholds any tangible rewards. Or, the superior may believe that a reward given at the present time might slow down a person's performance and hence he decides to withhold it until some future (perhaps indefinite) date. The point is, unless some potentially desirable outcome is actually given, or specifically promised, it cannot be considered a reward even though discriminations are made among different performers and rewards are available.

It was pointed out earlier that rewards can be intrinsic—provided by the person himself—as well as extrinsic. Intrinsic rewards thus involve the individual's feelings in relation to his task performance. If a manager feels he has obtained something valuable for himself, such as an increase in his knowledge, this is a reward, even though his boss or his company does not provide any additional desirable returns to him. The extent to which such intrinsic rewards are obtainable in the work situation will depend primarily on the way in which the job and tasks are structured by the organization. Frequently, intrinsic rewards will be accompanied by extrinsic rewards, but there clearly is no necessary reason for this to occur in every instance. Sometimes the individual will give himself an intrinsic reward even though others do not give him extrinsic rewards, and sometimes others will give him extrinsic rewards even though he himself feels that he has gained nothing intrinsically from performing the task.

Performance in Relation to Satisfaction

In our theoretical model, high performance will lead to high satisfaction only if it decreases the gap between the perceived equitable level of rewards and the amount seen as being actually received. Since a (self-rated) high performer probably would have relatively high expectations concerning an equitable level of rewards, this means, then, for a high performer to be satisfied he must receive rewards commensurate with his performance. If his rewards fail to live up to what he considers an equitable level for his performance, then he would be a relatively dissatisfied high performer.

Following the same line of reasoning, the model suggests how a low performer might be equally or even more satisfied than a given high performer. If a low performer has a low equitable level of rewards, and, in fact, receives a low level of rewards, the two values are close together; hence, he would be a "satisfied" employee by our definition. If, of course, the low performer has relatively high expectations concerning equitable rewards—a situation not untypical, since many low performers mistakenly believe that others consider them high performers—then he will be relatively dissatisfied.

From the foregoing it is possible to see why, for a given group of employees, performance may not be highly correlated with satisfaction. Since both the amount of rewards perceived as received and the perceived equitable level of rewards are involved in determining satisfaction, and since either or both of these amounts may, in fact, not be determined by performance *in a given situation,* we frequently would not expect a strong positive correlation between performance and satisfaction. One can quickly think of several different types of situations:

Situation #1: Rewards are associated positively with performance differences—i.e., higher performers get higher rewards—but the perceived levels of rewards are approximately the same for high and low performers. In this case, the higher performers would be more satisfied since their perceived rewards were close to their equitable rewards.

Situation #2: Rewards are associated positively with performance differences—i.e., higher performers get higher rewards—and the expected equitable levels of rewards are also in proportion to performance differences—i.e., higher performers expect more. In this situation, low performers would be as satisfied as high performers because the rewards they received were just as close to their expectations as was the case for the high performers.

Situation #3: Rewards are not related to performance differences— i.e., everybody gets about the same level of rewards—and the perceived equitable levels of rewards are approximately the same for high and low performers. Again, high and low performers would be about equally satisfied, since the differences between perceived equity and reality were about the same for the two groups.

Situation #4: Rewards are not related to performance differences— i.e., everybody gets about the same level of rewards—but the higher performers expect more. Here, high performers would be more dissatisfied than low performers because their equity-reality difference was larger than that of the low performers.

In the above hypothetical situations, the correlations between performance and satisfaction would be positive in Situation #1, close to zero in Situations #2 and #3, and negative in Situation #4. Quite clearly, we can see why performance and satisfaction are not highly positively correlated in most situations.

An aspect of the relationship between effort and performance should be mentioned here because of its relevance to the relationship between performance and satisfaction. Since effort does not lead directly to performance but is modified by abilities and role perceptions, ordinarily we should expect a weaker relationship between effort and satisfaction than between performance and satisfaction. Another way of saying this is that if organizations pay off directly in relation to performance levels, as they often claim they do, then performance should be more closely related than effort to satisfaction. On the other hand, if an organization rewards effort as much as or more than performance, then no such differentially weaker effort-satisfaction relationship should be found.

One further major point concerning the relationship of performance and satisfaction in our model concerns the direction of causality. We hypothesize that performance—through rewards, particularly intrinsic ones—has a more direct effect upon satisfaction than satisfaction has upon performance. In other words, *we see satisfaction primarily as a dependent variable* and not a causal variable. We do not exclude the possibility (even probability) that feelings of satisfaction can in turn influence future performance (see below). We do maintain, however, that such a connection is less direct than the reverse relationship. This is evident from the picture of the model which shows that the feedback loop involving satisfaction affecting performance is modified by more variables than is the connection forward from performance to satisfaction. To amplify this, let us turn to a consideration of "feedback relationships" in our model.

Feedback Relationships

Rewards in Relation to Effort-Reward Probability. One way for one's perception of the probability that reward depends upon effort to be increased is for one's performance to be rewarded commensurately. If a manager feels that his previous effort has resulted in rewards, then we would expect him to be more likely to feel that increased future effort will lead to increased future rewards. In this regard, it is necessary to stress two points: First, what the reward-giver considers to be rewards may not be so considered by the recipient and hence should not increase the probabilities in the recipient's mind that increased effort on his part will lead to increased rewards. Second, the reward recipient may not see the rewards as being connected with performance—that is why the feedback arrow starts from the performance-rewards connection and not from the rewards box—and, therefore, such rewards should not lead to increased perceived probabilities of effort leading to rewards. It is interesting to note that many organizations and superiors deceive themselves on both points and believe they should automatically get increased effort because they have "given something" to a subordinate. That is, what they have given and considered to be a "good" reward may not be thought of as much of a reward by the recipient. Even more important, perhaps, is the fact that although the recipient may be quite happy to obtain a given reward, he at the same time may see no connection between it and his performance. In this case his satisfaction should go up, but there would be very little, if any, effect on future performance. In a word, the organization has failed to make clear to the employee that the reward is being given as a direct result of a certain level of performance.

This hypothesized feedback loop from the performance-reward connection to the effort-reward probability is an especially important theoretical point, because of the failure of most expectancy theories to deal with past learning (see Chapter 1). This loop in our model implies that the way in which an organization rewards a manager following his performance will affect (for a given period of time) his perceptions of the connection of rewards to performance, which will, in turn, affect his expectancies that effort leads to rewards. To this extent, then, the model utilizes past learning experiences as a factor in determining expectancies about the future.

Satisfaction in Relation to Value of Reward. We hypothesize that when an individual feels satisfied after having received certain rewards, this will have an effect on the future values of rewards. From numerous psychological studies and from common observations, it is apparent that the satisfaction of certain basic needs temporarily reduces the value or attractiveness of rewards connected with these needs. Food is not highly valued just after a large meal is eaten. Water has no particular immediate value after thirst is quenched. Perhaps, even, when a person receives a very high level of monetary reward, this incentive will have a reduced value for at least a limited period of time. For other needs, however, the picture is not so clear (see Maslow, 1954). When a person receives recognition that lives up to his expected level of recognition, does this decrease the value or attractiveness of future recognition, or does it serve to increase the value? Research evidence is not definitive on this point. Our working hypothesis, not tested by the data we obtained, is that rewards associated with higher-order needs—such as esteem, autonomy, and self-actualization needs—become more attractive the more a person is rewarded and feels satisfied with a given level of rewards. At this point, the broadest statement we can make concerning the feedback loop from satisfaction to value of reward is that the effects of satisfaction on reward value may be different—even opposite—for different types of needs and their associated rewards.

CHAPTER 3

Methodology of the Study

RATIONALE OF METHODOLOGY

Researchers frequently distinguish between experimental studies and correlational studies when they discuss different research methods. An experimental study typically involves experimenter-produced changes in one variable in order to observe the effects on a second variable, while a correlational study focuses on the relationship between two variables without either of them being altered by the experimenter. The major disadvantage, from our point of view, of a correlational study is its inadequacy to prove directly the existence of the cause and effect relationships that are specified in a conceptual model. A correlational study can, however, establish whether two variables tend to be related at a fixed point in time. In terms of our study, if a close relationship were found as predicted, it would offer some support for our model; however, it does not establish that a cause and effect relationship exists. On the other hand, if no relationship were to be found where the model predicts that one should exist, then it is possible for a correlational study to disprove part of the model. Thus, correlational studies can sometimes disprove but never prove that a causal relationship exists. In effect, if they find no relationship, then experimental studies clearly are not warranted; but if they find relationships, they can suggest areas where experimental studies can profitably be done, experimental studies that will determine why the relationship found in the correlational study occurred.

The obvious problem with experimental studies in field research settings is that they require a high degree of cooperation by organizations in order to produce changes in variables and in order to control extraneous variables. Typically, this kind of cooperation is not feasible in business organizations. Further, experimental studies are limited in the number of variables they can consider. They can be expanded by adding more groups, and while this is often possible in the laboratory, it is seldom feasible in the field. After considering the relative advantages of the correlational and the experimental methods, it seemed that our purposes could best be served by a correlational study.

The present study is by necessity an exploratory one. It looks at an area where little previous research has been done, and, therefore, the format of the correlation study best fits the data we wished to obtain. The correlational approach makes it possible to look at a number of attitude variables relative to performance, and this is the crucial factor as far as testing the predictions of our model is concerned. Looking at all the relationships specified in the model with an experimental approach would require many studies—studies which may or may not be necessary in the future, depending upon the information that can be supplied in only one exploratory correlational study.

The type of question which is to be answered in a research project frequently limits the kind of research instruments that can be used in a study, and this is the case in the present study. The fact that the question we wished to focus on was one concerned with attitudes dictated the use of either questionnaires or interviews as the basic data collection instruments.

In deciding whether to use interviews or questionnaires, consideration was given to the kind of sample that we could expect to obtain with each method. Because we felt it would be possible to collect data from a larger and more heterogeneous sample if we used questionnaires, we decided to use this type of instrument to collect our data. It was felt that the advantages of obaining data from a cross section of management outweighed any benefits that might be gained from using interviews rather than questionnaires. One clear advantage of collecting data from a broad sample of management is an increased likelihood that the results of the study are not a function of the unique conditions existing in one company and are, therefore, more appropriate for generalization to other organizations. In effect, we made the decision to use questionnaires in order to obtain a broad sample while sacrificing the potential advantages that an interview might offer in the area of flexibility of questions and degree of involvement of the participating managers.

The choice of what type of measure of job performance to use was also largely determined by the topic of the study. Since we were interested in studying *managers'* attitudes and performance, many of the usual measures of job performance did not appear to be relevant. In most organizations there are, for example, typically no productivity or quality control records available for managers that would enable us to evaluate their performance "objectively." In addition, since we wanted to look at managers doing a wide variety of jobs, it became obvious that we would have to rely on ratings as our measure of job performance. The assumption was made that the superior and the manager himself were both in a reasonable position to evaluate the manager's performance, since they both should know about the job and the job performance.

It was also decided that global ratings (e.g., quality of job performance), rather than some composite of ratings on a number of specific traits, should be used. This decision was based partially upon Whitlock's (1963, 1965) impressive series of studies on the psychological basis of performance appraisals. His data suggest that when people are asked to make global ratings they act in a very predictable way, as efficient processors of critical-incident data from their observations of an individual's performance over the past six months. As Whitlock points out, judged quality of performance grows as a power function of the ratio of the number of specimens of effective to ineffective performance. Other studies have shown that raters tend to agree upon the weight to be assigned to the different behavior specimens; thus, high interrater reliability is possible. Basically, this suggests that simple global performance ratings may yield a reasonable approximation of what would be obtained by using a more extensive critical-incident or other type of check list. The factor analytic studies of ratings have also frequently produced a job performance factor.

In addition, Hollingworth's (1922) data on what traits can be rated reliably suggest that performance dimensions can be rated accurately. Thus, it seems that global performance ratings can be reliable and valid measures of behavior.

ATTITUDE MEASURES

The attitude data for the present study were obtained by the administration of two questionnaires. The first questionnaire focused upon managers' attitudes toward their pay. Specifically, this questionnaire contained attitude items relevant to four aspects of management compensation:
1. How pay is determined.
2. The importance of pay.
3. Satisfaction with the amount of pay received.
4. The degree to which pay functions as a satisfier (Herzberg *et al.*, 1959) .

The second questionnaire, which was distributed a month later as a follow-up to the initial questionnaire, focused upon two additional aspects of managerial jobs:
1. The type of role behavior required for success on the job.
2. The degee of need satisfaction provided by the job.

Appendix I contains a copy of the relevant parts of the first questionnaire, and Appendix II contains a complete copy of the follow-up questionnaire.

The questionnaires were distributed individually (either by company or by United States mail) to the members of management in each organization. Each of the first set of questionnaires was accompanied by a letter from the chief officer of the plant or division studied. In this letter the officer urged the manager to complete the questionnaire. However, it was pointed out that participation in the study was completely voluntary. The second set of questionnaires was accompanied by a personal letter from the researchers. In this letter the researchers thanked the managers for their cooperation in the first phase of the study and asked them to complete the second questionnaire as a final step in the research project. All questionnaires were numbered in order to identify the respondents; however, each manager was assured that his responses would be confidential. Along with the questionnaires and the letters, each respondent received a stamped, addressed envelope in which to return his completed questionnaire directly to the researchers at the university.

JOB BEHAVIOR MEASURES

Four measures of job behavior were obtained for each manager. Two of these measures were self-ratings that were obtained as part of the questionnaire concerned with attitudes toward pay. This questionnaire asked each manager to rate himself in relation to others with similar management duties on two factors: quality of job performance, and amount of effort put forth on the job. Appendix III contains a complete copy of the instructions and items used in obtaining these ratings. The two other measures of job performance were obtained by distributing a ranking form to the immediate superiors of all managers to whom the attitude questionnaires were distributed. These ranking forms were sent directly to the superiors along with a letter from an officer of the individual's organization assuring them that these rankings were to be used solely for research purposes. The ranking forms were distributed about two weeks after the first questionnaire was given to the managers. The superiors were provided with a return envelope and asked to return the forms directly to the researchers. These forms asked the superiors to rank their subordinates (the subordinates were listed by name on the forms) on the same two factors that the self-ratings were obtained on: how well managers were performing their jobs, and how much effort they were putting forth on their jobs. Appendix IV contains a complete copy of the ranking form that was distributed.

The obtained rankings were converted to standard scores for the purpose of the data analysis. This was accomplished by computing the percent position of each rank where:

$$\text{percent position} = 100 \ \frac{(N - \text{rank}) + 0.5}{N}$$

and then converting this figure into its standardized score equivalent by using a table of standardized score equivalents of percentile ranks in a normal distribution. This transformation is designed to yield scores with a mean of 50 and a standard deviation of 10.[1] This process assumes that the mean performance levels of the groups ranked by different managers are roughly equal. To the extent that this assumption is not met, there will be a tendency for the relationships between these performance measures and the other variables studied to be reduced.

Table 3–1 presents the Pearson product-moment correlation coefficients among the four job performance measures. These correlation coefficients indicate that there are substantial relationships between the two self-ratings and between the two superiors' rankings. That is, managers who rate themselves high on quality of job performance also rate themselves high on effort expended, and those managers who are rated high on quality of job performance by their superiors are also rated high by their superiors on effort expended. The sizes of these correlation coefficients (.47 and .59), however, indicate that the relationships are far from perfect. In the case of the two self-ratings, 25 percent of the variance is common to both ratings, and in the case of the two superiors' rankings, 35 percent of the variance is common to both rankings. This finding is in accord with the model presented in Chapter 2. The model pointed out that although effort expended is one factor that influences quality of job performance, it is not the only one. Thus, because of the influence of other factors (e.g., ability and role perceptions), the model does not predict a perfect relationship between effort expended and quality of job performance, and one is not found.

Table 3–1 also shows that the relationship between the self-ratings and the superiors' rankings of quality of job performance ($r = .03$), and the relationship between the self-ratings and the superiors' rankings of effort expended ($r = .20$), are disappointingly low. Undoubtedly, part of the cause of these low relationships can be traced to role perception differences between superiors and subordinates about what constitutes good job performance; also, certainly, some of it can be traced to a lack of reliability in both measures. Unfortunately, on the basis of the data collected for the present study, it is impossible to ascertain what

---

[1]The actual standard deviations were 8.01 for job performance and 8.11 for effort.

TABLE 3–1

Relationships among Measures of Job Performance
for the Total Sample ($N = 563$)

	Self-Rating of Job Performance	Self-Rating of Effort Expended	Superior's Ranking of Job Performance	Superior's Ranking of Effort Expended
Self-Rating of Job Performance	• • •	.47*	.03	.01
Self-Rating of Effort Expended	• • •	• • •	.11	.20*
Superior's Ranking of Job Performance ...	• • •	• • •	• • •	.59*
Superior's Ranking of Effort Expended	• • •	• • •	• • •	• • •

*$p < .01$

factors caused these relationships to be so low.[2] It is impossible to determine whether the self-ratings or the superiors' rankings represent the best assessment of an individual's job performance. Thus, rather than arbitrarily dismiss either set of ratings, it was decided to investigate the relationships between managers' attitudes and both the self-ratings and superiors' rankings of job performance.

Although neither the self-ratings nor the superiors' evaluations approach the kind of objective measurement that is typically desired, both are inherently interesting measures. The superiors' rankings are particularly significant, since it is on the basis of judgments like these that promotions, terminations, and salary increases are often made. The self-ratings are of interest because they represent one of the bases upon which individuals make decisions about remaining on the job, the adequacy of their pay,

---

[2]Although it is possible that either or both of these measures are simply invalid, this does not seem likely in the light of some other research evidence. For example, in another study (Lawler, 1967–b) in which the same performance measures were used, superiors' rankings of performance and effort were found to have convergent and discriminant validity when they were compared to peer rankings. This suggests that the superiors' ratings are probably valid.

and how hard to work. In short, self-ratings are one method that people use to determine the adequacy of their rewards in relation to their contributions to the organization. Individuals appear to evaluate their returns from their jobs—i.e., their pay and other rewards—according to their perceived inputs into the job (Adams, 1963). Included in their inputs are: how hard they work, how well they perform, and their qualifications. Obviously, this suggests that self-ratings are an important dimension that may affect both satisfaction and performance.

DESCRIPTION OF RESEARCH SITES

The present study was carried out in seven organizations. Three of the organizations (hereafter referred to as Organizations X, Y, and Z) are divisions of state governments and are subject to civil service policies. The other four organizations (hereafter referred to as Organizations A, B, C, and D) are privately owned manufacturing and utility companies.

Organization X is the employment department of a Western state government. The sample obtained from this organization was composed of managers of local employment offices. These managers typically had at least one level of supervision below them and were described by the state personnel department as lower-middle level managers. According to their job specifications, these managers are line supervisors who plan, select, direct, and organize the work of their subordinates.

Organization Y is the conservation department of a Western state government. This department contains the forestry department, the division of oil and gas, the division of mines, and the division of soil conservation. Data were collected from supervisors of local field or office groups in each of these divisions. Their duties are similar to those described for the department of employment sample (Organization X).

Organization Z operates state-owned retail liquor stores in a Southern state. Respondents for this study were the managers of the local stores. They had direct management responsibility for their stores and typically had an assistant manager as well as several clerks reporting to them.

Organization A is a large processer of canned foods. Managerial personnel from seven of the organization's processing plants were obtained for a sample for this study. Each plant contained a management force of about 17. The type of work, the number of employees supervised, and the hours of work varied widely for the management force because of the seasonal nature of the work. Each plant contained a personnel manager, an office manager, and several levels of line management.

Organization B is a large chemical manufacturer. Our investigation involved one plant in this organization. This plant contained a management force of about 70 and a total work force of about 1,000. The plant was engaged in the manufacture of several chemicals and could be considered a process production organization (Woodward, 1958). The present study collected data from all four levels of management in the plant, ranging from the plant manager down to first-level supervisors.

Organization C is a manufacturer and developer in the aerospace industry. The plant studied was located on the West Coast and employed more than 5,000 workers. The focus of the present study was on the two middle levels of management in a research and development department of the plant. Each manager supervised several small research and development groups.

Organization D is a geographically decentralized operating division of a large public utility. The division studied had a management force of about 110 with a work force of over 1,000 employees, and was largely devoted to performing service and maintenance work. The present study obtained a sample from all levels of management in the division. This ranged from the division superintendent down to the general foremen.

SAMPLE

The questionnaire concerned with attitudes toward pay was distributed to 635 managers in the seven organizations described above. Table 3–2 shows the response rates for each of these seven organizations. As can be seen from this table, all of the organizations had exceptionally high response rates, with the response rate of the total sample being 88.7 percent.

TABLE 3–2

Response Rates of the Seven Organizations
for the First Questionnaire (Pay)

Organization	Number of Questionnaires Distributed	Number of Questionnaires Returned	Percentage of Questionnaires Returned
X	87	80	92.0
Y	144	135	93.8
Z	27	22	81.5
A	110	91	82.7
B	68	63	92.6
C	88	69	78.4
D	111	103	92.8
Total Sample	635	563	88.7

The follow-up questionnaire, which was concerned with need satisfaction and role perceptions, was distributed to the same managers in Organizations X, A, B, C, and D who had previously received the pay questionnaire. Because of difficulties in distributing a second questionnaire to the managers in Organizations Y and Z, these organizations were not included in the second phase of the study. Table 3–3 shows the response rates for the five organizations that contributed samples for the follow-up questionnaire. As was true with the pay questionnaire, the response rate for the second questionnaire was high in all five organizations, with the overall response rate being 92.2 percent.

TABLE 3–3

Response Rates of the Five Organizations
for the Follow-up Questionnaire

Organization	Number of Questionnaires Distributed	Number of Questionnaires Returned	Percentage of Questionnaires Returned
X	87	85	97.7
A	110	106	96.4
B	68	58	85.3
C	88	76	86.4
D	111	103	92.8
Total Sample	464	428	92.2

Table 3-4 presents the demographic data characteristics of the respondents to the first questionnaire and of the respondents to the follow-up questionnaire. The high degree of similarity between the demographic characteristics of the two samples is due to the large amount of overlap in respondents between the two samples. Almost all of the managers who responded to the follow-up questionnaire had previously completed the first questionnaire.

TABLE 3-4

Characteristics of the Respondents to the First Questionnaire
and of the Respondents to the Follow-Up Questionnaire

	First Questionnaire	Follow-Up Questionnaire
N Lower Management[1]	274	250
N Middle Management[2]	289	178
Mean Age (Years)	45.0	44.8
Mean Seniority (Years)	17.2	17.7
Mean Time in Position (Years)	4.3	4.2
Education Level:		
% Having Beyond High School Degree	70.5	68.1
Average Annual Salary (Dollars) 11,325		11,500

[1]Lower management is defined as those managers who are on the lowest level of management in the organization and who generally were first line supervisors; typically, in the case of the present sample, they were white-collar supervisors rather than blue-collar foremen.

[2]Middle management is defined as consisting of those positions above the first level of supervision but below the vice-presidential company officer level.

Strictly speaking, neither of our samples of respondents is a random sample of American managers in general, and thus our conclusions must be restricted to the organizations studied. However, there are several factors that indicate the samples do represent a reasonable cross section of lower and middle level managers in American industry with the important exception that blue-collar foremen were not generally represented in the present study. First, the sample was drawn from organizations engaged in a wide variety of activities and centered in two different parts of the country. In addition, the organizations differed in size and in the type of organization structure employed. Thus, because of the variation in the characteristics of the organizations studied, there is little chance that any finding may be a function of conditions existing in a particular company or even a particular industry. Secondly, the high response rates obtained in all the organizations guarantee that an adequate sample of managers from each of these organizations was obtained. Finally, the demographic data characteristics of the sample, as shown in Table 3–4, are quite similar to the characteristics of previous broad samples of lower and middle level managers (Porter, 1961, 1962). This provides evidence that at least in terms of demographic characteristics the present sample is reasonably typical of middle and lower level management in general. Thus, because the sample does appear to be an adequate cross section of management, the results of the study may well generalize to a wide variety of organizations and individuals.

DESCRIPTION OF THE DATA ANALYSIS METHODS

The types of research questions considered in this project indicate that the data should be analyzed in a way that will allow us to determine if there exist consistent and statistically significant relationships between the attitude data and the performance data. There are two commonly used statistical methods for accomplishing this. One is to use a correlation coefficient to assess the degree of relationship between two variables, and the other is to divide the sample into high and low groups on the basis of one variable and then compare the scores of these high and low groups on a second variable. When this latter method of comparing high and low groups is used, the larger the difference between the groups on the second variable, the stronger is the relationship between the variables. The decision was made in the present study to use the method of comparing high and low groups in order to determine if relationships exist between or among variables in a way predicted by the model. Specifically, it was decided that a group comprising approximately the highest one third of scores on one variable should be compared with a group comprising approximately the bottom one third of scores on that variable. By looking at the top third and the bottom third it was hoped that two clearly different groups would be obtained. For example, the managers who made the performance rankings indicated that they had the greatest confidence in their ability to distinguish the best and the worst managers among their subordinates, but that it was difficult to separate the managers who were about average.

The high group versus low group comparison method has two advantages over the correlation coefficient method. One advantage has to do with the statistical assumptions required for the use of each method. The high versus low comparison approach makes fewer assumptions about the data, and thus seems to fit our own data better. For example, this method does not require, as correlation coefficients do, that both variables be scaled on equal interval scales. The second advantage has to do with the clarity with which the data can be communicated to the reader. The high versus low method allows the relationships to be presented in graphic form. Because of the complexity of the relationships involved in our study, it was felt that graphic representation would be the most meaningful way to communicate our results to the reader.

It should be noted that since both *t*-values and correlation coefficients are estimates of the proportion of variance accounted for, they are statistically comparable measures. As Hays (1963) points out, *t*-values, like correlation coefficients, indicate the proportion of the total variance in one variable that can be accounted for by knowing the other. Thus, by comparing two *t*-values that are based upon samples of similar size, it is possible to determine which of two relationships is stronger. A larger *t*-value reflects the fact that a stronger relationship exists between the two variables upon which it is based, than exists between the two variables upon which the smaller *t*-value is computed. This is an important point since at several places in our data analysis we will use *t*-values to illustrate the fact that two variables are more closely related to each other than are two other variables, or that two variables are more closely related to each other under one condition than under another condition. For our data, one variable will be the dimension upon which the sample is split into high and low groups, while a second variable will be the dimension upon which the two groups are compared.

In those cases where the strength of the relationship between two variables is compared with the strength of the relationship between two other variables, this can be evaluated statistically by testing for a significant difference between the mean differences. Typically in our data analysis, however, we decided not to report the data from the tests for the significance of differences between mean differences, despite the fact that in many instances they did reach statistical significance. This decision was based upon the fact that such differences are awkward to test for statistical significance and the fact that the level of statistical significance often was not crucial in terms of testing the model. Thus, raher than emphasize the results of any single test of significance of mean differences, we have chosen to emphasize the tendency for one difference to be consistently larger or smaller than another difference when similar data gathered from different situations are considered. In short, we have chosen to stress the consistency of the relationship between differences across samples, rather than their specific statistical significance levels, because of our feeling that this is a more meaningful indicator of the relationships in which we are interested.

It is common practice in presenting results graphically to place the independent variable on the X-axis and the dependent variable on the Y-axis. Thus, the mean score on the Y dimension is computed for subjects high, medium, and low on the X-axis. In the case of the present study, our theoretical model indicates that performance is both a dependent and an independent variable. Thus, performance must appear on the X-axis in some data analysis situations, and on the Y-axis in others. For example, in looking at perceptions about pay, attitudes toward how pay is determined will be on the X-axis, while performance will be on the Y-axis. However, when attitudes toward job satisfaction are considered, performance is seen as the independent variable, while satisfaction is seen as the dependent variable. Thus, in this latter case, mean satisfaction scores will be computed for high and low performance groups.

The difference between the mean scores of the high and low groups will be tested for statistical significance by means of t-tests. Where hypotheses were stated in advance, one-tail tests of significance are employed. The .05 level of confidence was accepted as the basis for rejecting the null hypothesis.

Because of the number of comparisons to be made in the present study, it is probable that some t-values will be significant by chance alone. It is particularly important, therefore, that the findings fit the overall pattern predicted by the model. Further, where possible, it will be important to determine if the same results appear in independent samples, thereby decreasing the probability that the significance of a finding is a mere chance occurrence. Thus, throughout the book we will often carry out the same data analyses for two independent populations in order to focus on the consistency of the findings.

CHAPTER 4

Attitudes toward Pay

"Pay is the most important single motivator in our organized society." (Haire *et al.*, 1963, p. 1).

"Wage systems are not in themselves an important determinant of pace of work, application to work, or output." (Brown, 1962, p. 15).

These two statements are typical of the contradictory claims about the effectiveness of pay as an incentive that abound in the literature on motivation and work. If we accept the former of these statements, pay should become the key building block in any scheme that attempts to motivate workers to perform their jobs better. If we accept the latter view, pay becomes a secondary motivational factor that needs only to be maintained at an adequate level. Unfortunately, the available empirical evidence is not very helpful in deciding which of these statements represents the more accurate view. The simple fact is that in relation to the importance of pay there is a paucity of evidence on how pay functions as an incentive.

It is surprising that business organizations have done so little research on the effectiveness of pay as an incentive. Salaries are one of the largest expenses for any organization, yet few organizations have attempted to assess systematically how effectively they are spending this money. Such disregard for how money is spent to purchase new machinery would be considered gross negligence; yet where salaries are concerned, it is overlooked.[1] But

[1]The authors are indebted to Mason Haire for this point.

if it is surprising that corporations have not studied pay more, it is even more curious that psychologists have failed to study the psychological aspects of compensation. As Haire *et al.* (1963) have pointed out, the basic assumption about pay—that it motivates people to work—is a psychological one. Its impact on employee behavior has many implications for any theory of human motivation. Thus, research on pay should have important practical as well as theoretical implications. However, psychologists have shown little interest in doing psychological research on pay in general, and on the relationship between attitudes toward pay and job performance in particular.

Despite the general lack of research on pay, it appears to be an ideal reward for us to study in order to begin to test our model. In contrast to many rewards, like status or security, it is measurable and thus lends itself rather easily to quantitatively oriented research. There is also a long history of attempts to use pay as a reward in order to increase er .loyee effort, and the analysis of this history would seem to provide a fruitful background against which to consider the implications of our model for the use of pay as an incentive. Knowledge about the relationship between attitudes toward pay and job performance would seem to be vital to an understanding of how pay can function as an incentive, as well as to an understanding of what kind of general theory of motivation may have validity for the work situation. Answers to such questions as (1) Does satisfaction with pay lead to higher job performance? and (2) Do an employee's attitudes about how his pay is determined influence his job performance? are crucial to an understanding of pay as an incentive, as well as to our theory, and can be found by studying the relationship between job attitudes and job performance.

HISTORICAL BACKGROUND

Prior to the "human relations" movement and the Western Electric studies, it was common to assume that pay was the only important incentive in the work environment. From this assumption grew a motivational picture of man that has since become known as "economic man." According to J.A.C. Brown (1954, pp. 15–16):

"Economic Man" is a rational, creative man who uses his reason primarily to calculate exactly how much satisfaction he may obtain from the smallest amount of effort. "Satisfaction" does not mean pride in one's job, the feeling of having accomplished something, or even the regard of others; it refers only to money.

With this concept of man in mind, organizations began in the early 1900's frantically installing various kinds of pay plans. Hundreds of different plans were tried and some attempts were made to measure the resulting changes in productivity. However, these incentive plans typically failed to live up to expectations. Although it is generally conceded that they frequently produced performance increases that ranged from 10 to 40 percent, they also produced many human relations problems (Whyte, 1955), including quota restrictions and "goldbricking." During this entire period little attention was focused on developing a theoretical model that would explain why some schemes succeeded while others failed, and why the many unexpected side effects appeared when incentive plans were installed.

A general growing disillusionment with incentive plans and the concept of "economic man" set the stage for the acceptance of the results of the Western Electric studies (Roethlisberger and Dickson, 1939). These studies clearly demonstrated that factors other than financial ones influence an individual's productivity. For Elton Mayo, the most important of these other factors was the individual's social relations on the job. Soon a picture of motivation that can be called "social man" appeared and the "human relations" movement came into prominence. Mayo (1945) perfectly characterizes "social man" with the statement that "man's desire to be continuously associated with his fellows is a strong, if not the strongest, human characteristic." The developing "human relations" movement apparently contributed to the abandonment of many incentive pay plans. In 1935 (pre-"human relations") 75 percent of a sample of companies replied that they used wage incentive programs. By 1939 (beginning of "human relations") the number had fallen to 52 percent and by 1958 the number had declined to 27 percent. Motivational schemes during this period were frequently designed in a way that essentially ignored the use of pay as a motivator, despite the fact that the Western Electric studies themselves found that in the Second Relay Assembly room a substantial increase in productivity was due to the wage incentive system.

"Social man" was not due to last too long, for soon Maslow (1943, 1954) presented a theory of motivation that introduced "self-actualizing" man. For many, Maslow's theory provided a meaningful explanation of why incentive systems had failed and of why pay may lack primary importance for employees in our society. Briefly, Maslow's theory says that the needs which individuals seek to satisfy are arranged in a hierarchy. At the bottom of the hierarchy are needs for food, water, and physical comfort. These lower order needs are followed by such higher order needs as social needs, esteem needs, and finally, needs for autonomy and self-actualization. According to Maslow's theory, once the lower order needs are relatively well satisfied, they become unimportant as motivators, and an individual tries to satisfy the higher order needs. If it is assumed, as many advocates of self-actualizing man do, that pay primarily satisfies lower order needs, then the reason for the failure of incentive systems becomes clear. In our society, lower order needs are well satisfied for most individuals, and thus one would not expect pay to be important. This kind of explanation argues that most pay plans have failed because pay is unimportant, and, as our model points out, pay cannot be a motivator if it is unimportant. But—and this is the key point—this view is based upon the assumption that pay satisfies mainly lower order needs. There are real questions concerning the validity of this assumption.

RESEARCH STUDIES ON PAY

Recent studies have shown rather clearly that pay is an incentive that is able to satisfy both lower order physiological and security needs as well as higher order needs such as esteem and recognition (Lawler and Porter, 1963; Myers, 1964). It is this very facet of pay that suggests it as a particularly appropriate reward to look at in relation to our model. Pay is one reward that does satisfy a variety of important needs, and our expectation is that rewards seem to gain their value as a function of their ability to satisfy needs. For this reason, it would seem that if our expectations about the way outcomes gain reward value are at all valid, pay should be an ideal reward to study in order to test our arguments concerning the impact of rewards on behavior.

The results of several recent studies support the point that pay remains important to managers despite their relatively high standing in terms of lower order need satisfactions. Porter (1961) found that managers attached more importance to the amount of pay they received than to the amount of autonomy, esteem, or social need fulfillment they received. Lawler and Porter (1963) found that although presidents and vice presidents attached slightly less importance to their pay than did lowel level managers, the difference was small, and for both groups it was rated as very important. What probably does change as managers earn more money is the type of needs satisfied by money and consequently the reasons it is important to them.

In summary, although pay may be important to people for a number of reasons, and may be of differing amounts of importance to individuals depending on their needs at that moment, it is clear that pay is important enough in most instances to be a significant motivator of behavior. One example of the strength of pay as an incentive is given by a recent Labor Department report. According to the report, the longshoremen at the Port of Galveston, Texas, work too hard. The report said, "It cannot be in the best interests of the health of the men to carry on hard physical labor at such a pace all day, much less day after day." The reason for the hard work was found in the incentive pay system under which the men worked. According to the report, the men could earn as much as $6 to $10 an hour under their incentive system, which effectively tied their pay to their job performance. It is obvious that this story of a workable incentive plan is not an isolated example. Even the early plans got some improvement in productivity, and later ones like the Scanlon Plan have had a number of successes. Perhaps the most successful plan has been the one used at the Lincoln Electric Company. It has resulted in the company having sales per employee that are approximately four times the industry average.

The crucial empirical question about pay as a motivator of job performance is not the traditional one of, "Are incentive plans efficient motivators of effective job performance?" but the differential one of, "Under what conditions is pay a significant motivator of effective job performance?" Such a question pertains directly to our conceptual model. One way to answer this differential question is by comparing effective managers' attitudes about pay with those of ineffective managers. Our model makes it clear that there are two such kinds of attitudes that are needed among employees if pay is to function as an incentive. According to the model, pay must be important to the individual, and the individual must see a positive connection between his attempts to perform well and his pay in both the short and long term. If either of these two attitudes is lacking, then pay will not be an effective incentive; and no relationship would be expected between how important pay is, or how it is determined, and performance.

PROBLEMS WITH EARLY INCENTIVE PLANS

It is quite possible that the ineffectiveness of many of the early incentive plans can be attributed to their failure to establish a clear relationship between performance and pay. Rate changes have destroyed employees' beliefs that good performance does lead to high pay, and the fear of unemployment because of overproducing has tended to undermine workers' perceptions that their long-term economic good is fostered by high performance. Whyte (1955) has shown that such fears may be widespread among workers in industry, and that they do reduce the effectiveness of incentive pay plans. More recently, Chalupsky (1964) found that in a group of research organizations only 67 percent of the scientists said merit salary increases existed, despite the fact that management claimed they were present in all the organizations. Thus, it is not only among blue-collar workers that incentive plans may fail because a clear relationship between pay and performance does not exist.

There is some evidence that pay programs also may have failed because money is relatively unimportant to some employees despite the fact that a clear relationship is seen between pay and performance. However, there is no evidence that this reason is as widespread as the advocates of "social man" and of "self-actualizing man" would lead one to believe by their tendency to ignore pay. Perhaps the most striking example of a situation where pay was not a valued reward was in a factory where the employees were mostly young girls who lived at home with their parents. Since they had to give their pay envelopes to their mothers, the amount of their pay was of relatively little importance to them, and increased pay proved to be a poor incentive. On the other hand, the chance to leave work early if all the work was completed proved to be an effective incentive.

A further reason why incentive plans may fail, and one that is congruent with our model, is this: although pay may be regarded as important, and good job performance may be seen as leading to higher pay, good job performance *also* may be seen as leading to a reduction in other rewards. It is not at all uncommon to find situations in which such needs as esteem and friendship from fellow employees are withheld from the good job performer or "ratebuster." Thus, the significant positive motivational effects of seeing a valued reward—pay—increased by improved job performance may be canceled out by the negative effects of seeing other valued rewards decreased by improved job performance.

HYPOTHESES

Confirmation of the prediction that seeing a close connection between pay and performance will lead to good performance was indicated in a study by Georgopoulos, Mahoney, and Jones (1957). They found that workers who rated themselves highly tended to see good performance as helpful in obtaining higher pay. Thus, on the basis of our model and the evidence of the Georgopoulos *et al.* study, it is possible to state our first hypothesis about the kinds of attitudes toward pay that should be associated with high effort to perform effectively.

Hypothesis 4–A. The higher the perceived probability that pay depends upon job performance factors, the more effort an individual will devote to performing his job effectively.[2]

It is important to note in Hypothesis 4–A that the relationship predicted is one between attitudes and the amount of effort de-

---

[2] ". . . the perceived probability that pay depends upon job performance factors" refers to the following specific probabilities: that pay depends upon effort, that pay depends upon quality of job performance, and that pay depends upon productivity.

voted to performing effectively. As the model points out, the degree to which this effort is effectively converted into performance will be a function of the individual's ability as well as his role perceptions. This means that effort will not bear a perfect relationship to quality of job performance, a fact that would tend to reduce the relationship between the attitudes and quality of job performance. Thus, on the basis of the relationship between effort and performance stated in our model, it is possible to state our second hypothesis:

Hypothesis 4–B. Attitudes about the perceived probability that pay depends upon job performance factors will be more closely related to the amount of effort an individual devotes to his job than to the quality of his job performance.

Our model stresses that attitudes about the perceived probability that pay depends upon job performance factors will predict effectively about job behavior only where pay is important to the employees. Partial support for this view comes from the Georgopoulos *et al.* study, which found that the relationship between attitudes toward how pay is determined and job performance was strongest for those employees who rated pay high in importance. Somewhat similar results were also found in a recent study by Galbraith (1966). Thus, on the basis of the Georgopoulos *et al.* and the Galbraith studies and our model, we can state our third hypothesis:

Hypothesis 4–C. The relationship between the perceived probability that pay depends upon job performance factors and measures of actual performance and effort will be stronger for those individuals who say their pay is important to them than it will be for those who say their pay is relatively unimportant to them.

It should be noted that hypotheses 4–A, 4–B, and 4–C do not differentiate between the perceived probability that effort leads to pay and the perceived probability that performance leads to pay, in terms of the strength of their relationship to the performance measures. We noted in Chapter 2 that the key perceived probability was the one concerned with the degree to which pay is seen as depending upon effort. This argument was developed because it was felt that the perception that pay depends upon effort combines the two important perceptions of pay depending upon performance and performance depending upon effort. The assumption was that the perception that pay depends upon performance is only one component of the perception that effort leads to pay, and therefore it should not be as good a predictor of actual effort expended and actual performance as is the perception that pay depends upon effort. On the basis of this reasoning we can state our fourth hypothesis:

Hypothesis 4–D. The perceived probability that pay depends upon effort will be more highly related to measured actual job performance and effort than will be the perceived probability that pay depends upon quality of job performance.

A widely discussed book by Herzberg, Mausner, and Snyderman (1959) has also considered the relationship between attitudes toward pay and job performance. The Herzberg *et al.* theory of motivation classifies job factors into two groups, one of which is called satisfiers and the other dissatisfiers. According to the theory, satisfiers, or motivators, as they have been labeled more recently, have the power to motivate outstanding job performance. Dissatisfiers, or maintenance factors, as they are often referred to, can only serve to restrict productivity and interfere with it if they are not at an adequate level. Herzberg *et al.* further state that satisfiers can only contribute to job satisfaction, and that they tend to be associated with particularly gratifying experiences. Examples of these are achievement, recognition, advancement, and responsibility. Dissatisfiers, on the other hand, can only contribute to job dissatisfaction if they are particularly poor or if in some way conditions are not "hygienic." Examples of these factors are working conditions, company policies, and supervision. Pay, interestingly, appeared about equally as a satisfier and as a dissatisfier in the data collected, although in a somewhat circuitous interpretation of their results Herzberg *et al.* classified it as a dissatisfier.

Since 1959 a great deal of research has been directed toward testing the facet of the Herzberg *et al.* theory concerned with distinguishing which factors contribute to job satisfaction and which to dissatisfaction. A number of studies have addressed themselves to the question of, "Are there certain job factors that contribute only to dissatisfaction while others contribute only to satisfaction?" The results of these studies have provided mixed support for the Herzberg *et al.* theory. Studies by Myers (1964) and Schwartz, Jenusaitis, and Stark (1963) have offered some support, while others (e.g., Wernimont, 1964; Dunnette *et al.*, 1967) have failed to support the theory. Thus, although a considerable amount of research has been directed at this aspect of the Herzberg theory, the question of its validity remains in doubt at this time.

Significantly, while considerable research has been focused on which factors contribute to satisfaction and dissatisfaction, little attention has been focused on testing the *performance* implications of the theory. The original study by Herzberg asked the subjects (engineers and accountants) to report how the job factors affected their performance. The finding was that satisfiers boosted performance while dissatisfiers reduced it. Overall, satisfiers seemed to have the strongest impact upon performance. At best, this is weak evidence that attitudes are related to performance, since only self-reports were used, and in many cases the managers were reporting on events that had happened a considerable length of time prior to the time of their interviews. But this evidence, although not at all conclusive, is at least suggestive of the kinds of attitudes that might be associated with effective job performance. Since virtually none of the studies that have attempted to test the theory have been concerned with performance aspects, this part of the theory in particular needs further investigation.

Of specific interest for the present study were the kinds of attitudes toward pay in the Herzberg *et al.* study that were seen by the respondents to lead to high performance. Although salary tended to appear as both a satisfier and a dissatisfier, it was mentioned in a special way when it appeared as a satisfier and contributor to good performance. Specifically, it was mentioned as something that went along with a person's achievement on the job. "It was a form of recognition; it meant that the individual was progressing in his work." Thus in these situations, pay appeared to be satisfying higher- as well as lower-order needs.

How, then, do the Herzberg pay attitude data fit our model? According to the model, the only attitudes that lead to effective job performance are those that indicate the individual sees signif-

icant rewards as contingent upon good job performance. Statements such as "pay is a form of recognition" or "it meant an
individual was doing his job well," that were typical of people in
the Herzberg study who saw pay as a satisfier, seem to be in part
saying that pay, recognition, and achievement are seen as being
tied to performance. Seeing pay as a satisfier, therefore, apparently
means seeing such important rewards as recognition, pay, and
achievement as contingent upon job performance. It is not surprising, therefore, that in the Herzberg study the effective performers were those who saw their pay as a satisfier or, in terms of
our model, those who saw their pay and other rewards as dependent upon their own efforts to perform well. Interpreted this
way, the results of the Herzberg study with respect to pay and
performance appear to be congruent with and, in fact, predictable
from our theory. Thus, on the basis of the results of the Herzberg
et al. study and our model, we can state our first hypothesis relative to pay as a satisfier:

Hypothesis 4–E. The more an individual sees his pay as a satisfier, the
more effort he will put forth to perform his job effectively.

As is pointed out in Hypothesis 4–E, attitudes toward pay as a
satisfier are assumed to be attitude reflections of how hard an
individual will work, rather than necessarily the actual quality
of his job performance. Thus, because of the relationship between
effort and performance, it is possible to state a second hypothesis
about the relationship between attitudes toward pay as a satisfier
and performance:

Hypothesis 4–F. Attitudes toward the degree to which pay is seen as a
satisfier will be more closely related to the amount of effort an individual
puts forth on his job than to the quality of his job performance.

The model predicts that the relationship between attitudes
toward the perceived probability that pay depends upon performance and job performance will be stronger for those managers
to whom pay is important than for those to whom it is unimportant (Hypothesis 4–C). Since attitudes toward pay as a satisfier seem to express partly the degree to which pay is tied to
performance, the same relationship might be expected to hold for
them. That is, the relationship between attitudes toward pay as a

satisfier and effective performance will be strongest for those managers who say pay is important to them. Although this seems like a reasonable hypothesis, it should be pointed out that seeing pay tied to performance is not identical to seeing it as a satisfier.

Hypothesis 4–G. The relationship between an individual's attitudes toward pay as a satisfier and measures of actual performance and effort will be stronger for those managers who say their pay is important to them than for those who say their pay is relatively unimportant to them.

PAY PROGRAMS OF THE ORGANIZATIONS STUDIED

The three government organizations studied were all under civil service compensation systems, and thus were subject to similar pay programs. In these organizations, pay ranges were established for each job, and the ranges for all jobs were known by all employees. Further, most individuals holding similar jobs received the maximum pay possible for that position, regardless of individual merit. The only managers who did not receive the maximum pay for their jobs were those recently promoted managers who, because of lack of seniority or experience, could not qualify for the top pay grade. Merit, of course, was a factor in determining who was promoted to higher-level jobs, and it did have an indirect effect on the managers' pay. However, the majority of the raises received by these managers were based upon cost-of-living increases and not on merit. Thus, for these government organizations, job level, seniority, and experience were the most important and direct determinants of managers' pay.

The four privately owned organizations that were studied all had relatively similar management compensation programs. As was true with the government organizations, each job had a pay range. However, this was the only point of similarity between the pay programs of the private and government organizations. The four private organizations maintained policies of strict secrecy with regard to both individuals' pay and the pay ranges for management jobs. Further, all the organizations had control points in their range systems that prevented all but a few of the managers in the organization from reaching the top of the pay range for a given job. The purpose of this control point was to make merit an important factor in determining individual managers' pay. Of course, as was true in the government, seniority was also an important criterion for obtaining higher pay. The pay policy of Organization C differed slightly from the policies of the other private organizations considered. Because of the highly technical field in which it operated, Organization C was forced to put considerable emphasis upon education and technical knowledge in determining managers' compensation. In none of the four organizations was a year-end merit bonus an important factor in determining the individual's pay level. Thus, for all the industrial organizations, with the possible exception of Organization C, merit and job level appeared to be the most important determinants of the managers' pay.

Because of the great similarities among the pay policies of the three government organizations, it was decided to combine the data obtained from these organizations. Therefore, in all the data analyses concerned with attitudes toward pay, the data gathered from Organizations X, Y, and Z will be combined and treated as a single government sample. Similarly, because of the relative similarities among the pay policies of the private organizations, the pay attitude data gathered from Organizations A, B, C, and D will be combined and treated as a single private industry sample.

There are several advantages to analyzing the data from the government sample and from the private industry sample separately. First, it allows for testing of all hypotheses in two independent samples. Second, it allows us to view the impact of these two different types of pay programs and to make comparisons between the effects of the two programs.

ATTITUDE MEASURES OBTAINED

Perceived Probability that Pay Depends upon Job Performance Factors

Each respondent was asked to rate how important his organization considered each of nine factors to be in determining his pay. Each factor was followed by a seven-point scale with the adjective "important" corresponding to the number seven on the scale and "unimportant" to the number one. Three of these nine factors were designed to measure the amount of importance the respondent felt was attached to job performance factors in determining his pay, or, in terms of the model, the perceived probability that job performance factors influence pay. Table 4–1 lists the three items used, as well as the degree of relationship among them as measured by Pearson product-moment correlation coefficients.[3]

TABLE 4–1

Correlations among Items Designed to Measure the
Managers' Perception of the Importance of Job
Performance Factors in Determining Their Pay

		Government Sample		Private Sample	
		Q. 6	Q. 7	Q. 6	Q. 7
Question 5	Quality of Job Performance	.80*	.66*	.71*	.50*
Question 6	Productivity on the Job		.67*		.61*
Question 7	Amount of Effort Expended on the job ..				

*$p < .01$

The intercorrelations among the items in both samples are high, indicating that there is a large degree of homogeneity among the items. These correlations would appear to be particularly high since they approach the limits set by the typical test-retest reliability of these types of items. The model points out that the probability that effort will lead to rewards is a product of the probability that effort will lead to performance and the probability that performance will lead to the reward. This led us to expect a somewhat lower correlation among these items. Judging from the high correlations actually found in the present study, it appears that these managers did not tend to distinguish between the probability that effort leads to pay and the probability that performance leads to pay. This would indicate that for them the concern about whether effort was likely to result in performance was not a major consideration, and that the major concern was whether performance would result in pay. In the case of the pres-

---

[3]Appendix I contains a complete copy of this part of the questionnaire.

ent study it was decided, because of the high intercorrelations among the three items, to create a composite index of the perceived probability that pay depends upon job performance factors. This index has the obvious advantage, from a measurement point of view, of greater reliability than that of any single item because of the added length. This index was created by summing each manager's responses to the three job performance items. The higher a manager scored on this index, the higher the perceived probability that for him pay depends upon job performance factors.

Pay as a Satisfier

The degree to which the managers saw their pay as a satisfier was measured by three items. The managers were asked to indicate their agreement or disagreement with each of the three items on a five-point Likert-type scale. The three relevant items were embedded among other questions concerned with attitudes toward pay. Table 4–2 presents the items as well as the degree of relationship among them as measured by Pearson correlation coefficients.[4]

TABLE 4–2

Correlations among Items Measuring Degree
to Which Pay Is Seen as a Satisfier

		Government Sample		Private Sample	
		Q. 4	Q. 6	Q. 4	Q. 6
Question 2	For me, raises have meant that I was progressing in my work	.64*	.49*	.61*	.52*
Question 4	The raises I have received were rewards for good performance		.61*		.65*
Question 6	In my job, pay is a form of recognition for a job well done				

*p < .01

The intercorrelations among the items are substantial, indicating that there is a high degree of homogeneity among the items.

[4]Appendix I contains a complete copy of this part of the questionnaire.

This is desirable, since it suggests that the items are reliable, and it makes it possible to combine the items into a meaningful composite measure of "pay as a satisfier." Such an index of pay as a satisfier was computed for each subject by summing his score on the three items. The higher the score on this index of pay as a satisfier, the more pay is seen as a satisfier.

Reward Value

One item that contained three parts was included to measure satisfaction with pay and the reward value of pay. The specific item was as follows:

The *pay* for my management position
   a) How much *is there now?*
   b) How much *should there be?*
   c) How *important* is this to me?

The managers were asked to respond to parts *a*, *b*, and *c* on a scale running from 1 (minimum) to 7 (maximum). Satisfaction was measured by subtracting a manager's response to *a* from his response to *b*. The greater this difference, the greater is the *dis*satisfaction. The data gathered from this measure will be considered in Chapter 7, which is concerned with the relationship between pay satisfaction and performance. The answer to part *c* constituted a measure of the perceived importance or reward value of pay, and is necessary to test the hypotheses concerned with pay as a satisfier and with attitudes toward how pay is determined.[5]

TESTS OF THE HYPOTHESES

Hypothesis 4–A stated that the higher the perceived probability that job performance factors influence pay, the more effort an individual will put forth in attempting to perform his job effectively. In order to test this hypothesis, we will present only the data on the relationship between the composite index of the perceived probability that pay depends upon job performance and the measures obtained on the managers' actual job behavior (i.e., the self and superiors' ratings on both effort

---

[5]Appendix I contains a complete copy of this part of the questionnaire.

and quality of job performance). Later we will consider the relationship between each of the three perceived probabilities that make up the composite index and these same job behavior measures.

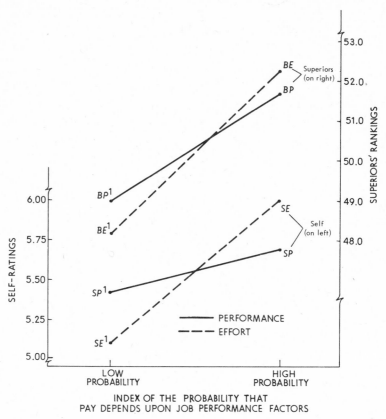

Figure 4–1. Mean self (S) and superiors' (B) ratings of job performance and effort for high and low probability attitude groups (Private Industry Sample).

N: BP[1] $= 98$; BP $= 108$; BE[1] $= 100$; BE $= 109$; SP[1] $= 106$; SP $= 119$; SE[1] $= 106$; SE $= 119$. Comparisons—BP[1](49.0) vs. BP(51.7): $t = 2.16$, $p < .05$. BE[1] (48.2) vs. BE(52.3): $t = 3.28$, $p < .01$. SP[1](5.4) vs. SP(5.7): $t = 1.53$, n.s. SE[1](5.1) vs. SE(6.0): $t = 4.63$, $p < .01$.

Figures 4–1 and 4–2 present the relevant data for hypothesis 4–A. For these figures, the composite index is represented on the X-axis in the form of groups low and high on this variable. The Y-axis represents the rated behavior of the managers. The scale for the self-ratings (the two lower lines on the figures) is on the left, and the scale for the superiors' ratings (the two upper lines on the figures) is on the right. Thus, for hypothesis 4–A to be supported, the high groups should have higher scores on the effort measures on the Y-axis than should the low groups. Such a finding would be represented by lines in the figure that increased going from left to right.

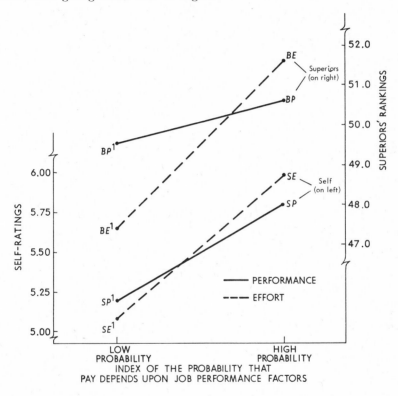

Figure 4–2. Mean self and superiors' ratings of job perfomance and effort for high and low probability attitude groups (Government Sample).
N: $BP^1 = 74$; $BP = 57$; $BE^1 = 74$; $BE = 57$; $SP^1 = 85$; $SP = 61$; $SE^1 = 85$; $SE = 61$. Comparisons—$BP^1(49.5)$ vs. $BP(50.6)$: $t = .72$, n.s. $BE^1(47.4)$ vs. $BE(51.6)$: $t = 2.65$, $p < .01$. $SP^1(5.2)$ vs. $SP(5.8)$: $t = 3.16$, $p < .01$. $SE^1(5.1)$ vs. $SE(6.0)$: $t = 5.13$, $p < .01$.

Figure 4–1 presents the data from the private sample. It shows that there is a clear and consistent tendency for those managers who feel that there is a high probability that their job performance is important in determining their pay to be rated higher on both quality of job performance and effort expended, than are those managers who feel their job performance is relatively unimportant in determining their pay. The two upper lines in Figure 4–1 show that this finding holds for the self-ratings. Three of these four differences are significant at the .05 level.

Figure 4–2 presents the same type of results shown in Figure 4–1, except that it contains the data from the government sample. The results for the government sample are similar to those found in the private sample. The more managers feel their pay is dependent upon their performance, the higher they are rated on the two job behavior measures (effort and quality of job performance). In the government sample, three of the four performance differences between the high and low groups are significant at the .05 level. As was true in the private sample, in all cases the job behavior scores of the high group are always higher than those of the low group. Thus, the data from both the private and government samples indicate that those managers who are rated high on effort expended and on quality of job performance see the greatest probability that their pay is dependent upon job performance factors. Particularly, the strong findings with respect to the ratings of effort would appear to offer strong support for Hypothesis 4–A.

Hypothesis 4–B stated that attitudes about the degree to which pay is seen to depend upon job performance factors will be more closely related to the amount of effort an individual devotes to his job than to the quality of his job performance. The data presented in both Figures 4–1 and 4–2 are relevant for this hypothesis. Figure 4–1 shows that the lines representing the relationship between the ratings on effort and the probability attitudes are steeper than those representing the relationship between the ratings on job performance and the attitudes. Thus, there is a larger difference between the high and low probability groups on the ratings of effort than upon the ratings of performance. (As was pointed out before, the larger the difference between the high and low attitude groups, the stronger is the relationship between the behavior measure and the attitudes.) The larger *t*-values for the effort ratings than for the performance ratings also reflect the fact that a stronger relationship exists between the attitudes and effort than between the attitudes and quality of job performance. For example, the difference between the high and low attitude groups is significant on the self-ratings of effort but is not significant on the self-ratings of performance.

The data in Figure 4–2 show that the same tendency exists for the data collected from the government sample as existed for the private sample. Again, the larger differences between the high and low probability attitude groups come from the ratings of effort rather than from the ratings of quality of job performance. Thus, for both the private and the government samples, the differences between the high and low attitude groups are greater on both the self and the superiors' ratings of effort than they are on the comparable ratings of performance. The evidence, therefore, consistently tends to support the validity of Hypothesis 4–B.

Hypothesis 4–C stated that the relationship between the probability that pay is dependent upon job performance and actual job behavior will be stronger for those managers who rate pay as important than for those who rate it as relatively unimportant. Figures 4–3, 4–4, 4–5, and 4–6 present the data relevant to this hypothesis. The hypothesis was tested by first dividing the managers into high and low importance groups on the basis of their answer to the question (part c of the satisfaction question) which asked how important their pay was to them. Then, they were divided into high and low perceived probability groups. Figure 4–3 compares the high and low importance groups from the private sample on the ratings of performance. As can be seen for both the self and the superior ratings of job performance, there is a stronger relationship between performance and the probability attitudes for the high than for the low importance group. This is shown in the figure by the steeper slope of the line representing the high importance group and the consequent larger difference on performance between the high and low probability attitude groups. Also, the t-values are significant for the high importance groups but not for the low importance groups, further supporting the hypothesis.

The data presented in Figure 4–4 show that the same results as were found in the private sample tend to hold in the government sample. Figures 4–5 and 4–6 show that the results that held for the self and superiors' ratings on performance also hold for the ratings on effort. Again, stronger relationships appear for the high than for the low importance groups.

Looking at all four figures, there are eight comparisons between high and low importance groups, and in each comparison the difference between the high and low probability attitude groups is larger for the high importance than for the low importance

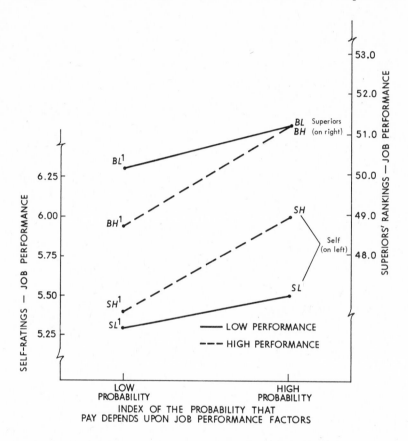

Figure 4-3. Mean self and superiors' ratings of job performance for high and low probability groups with two levels of pay importance (Private Industry Sample).

N: $BL^1 = 36$; $BL = 47$; $BH^1 = 57$; $BH = 51$; $SL^1 = 38$; $SL = 49$; $SH^1 = 66$; $SH = 58$. Comparisons—$BL^1(50.1)$ vs. $BL(51.2)$: $t = .53$, n.s. $BH^1(48.7)$ vs. $BH(51.2)$: $t = 2.18$, $p < .05$. $SL^1(5.3)$ vs. $SL(5.5)$: $t = 1.10$, n.s. $SH^1(5.4)$ vs. $SH(6.0)$: $t = 2.90$, $p < .01$.

groups. In all eight cases, the difference between the high and low attitude groups is statistically significant for the high importance groups, but in only four cases is it significant for the low importance groups. Thus, since the data from both samples and from both the superiors' and the self-ratings are in agreement with the hypothesis, it seems reasonable to conclude that Hypothesis 4–C is substantiated by our data.

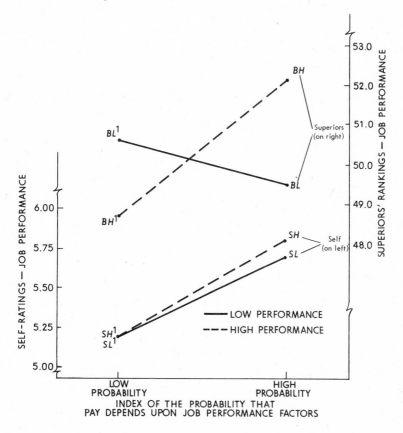

Figure 4–4. Mean self and superiors' ratings of job performance for high and low probability groups with two levels of pay importance (Government Sample).
  N: $BL^1 = 29$; $BL = 30$; $BH^1 = 41$; $BH = 36$; $SL^1 = 34$; $SL = 36$; $SH^1 = 46$; $SH = 36$. Comparisons—$BL^1(50.6)$ vs. $BL(49.5)$: $t = .58$, n.s. $BH^1(48.7)$ vs. $BH(52.1)$: $t = 1.70$, $p < .05$. $SL^1(5.2)$ vs. $SL(5.7)$: $t = 2.40$, $p < .05$. $SH^1(5.2)$ vs. $SH(5.8)$: $t = 2.61$, $p < .01$.

It is important to note that if Hypotheses 4–B and 4–C are considered together, then the strongest relationship between the job behavior ratings and the degree to which pay is seen to be dependent upon performance should come on the ratings of effort

for the high importance groups. The results presented in Figures
4–3 through 4–6 show that this is exactly what happened. For example, on the superiors' rankings of effort for the high pay importance group of managers, the difference between the high and
low probability attitude groups is 5.9 in the private sample

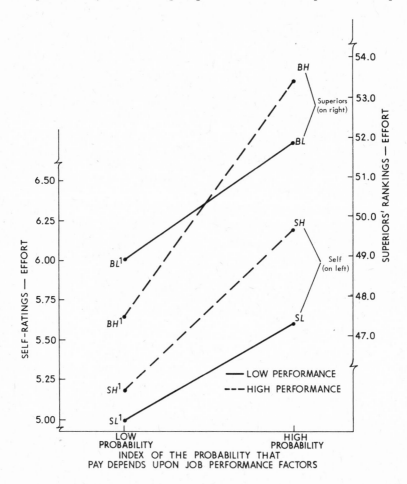

Figure 4–5. Mean self and superiors' ratings of effort for high and low
probability groups with two levels of pay importance (Private Industry
Sample).

N: BL¹ = 36; BL = 47; BH¹ = 57; BH = 52; SL¹ = 38; SL = 49; SH¹ = 60;
SH = 58. Comparisons—BL¹(49.0) vs. BL(51.8): $t = 1.42$, n.s. BH¹(47.5) vs. BH
(53.4): $t = 3.48$, $p < .01$. SL¹(5.0) vs. SL(5.6): $t = 3.23$, $p < .01$. SH¹(5.2) vs. SH
(6.2): $t = 4.65$, $p < .01$.

(Figure 4–5) and 4.2 in the government sample (Figure 4–6). However, for the low importance group of managers, the difference on the superiors' ranking of quality of job performance between the high and low groups is 1.1 for the private sample (Figure 4–3) and − 1.1 for the government sample (Figure 4–4). Similarly, for the self-ratings, there is a large difference between

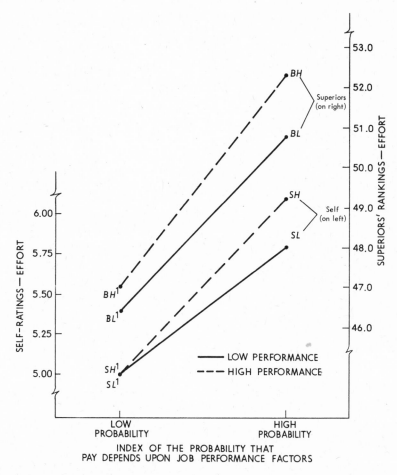

Figure 4–6. Mean self and superiors' ratings of effort for high and low probability groups with two levels of pay importance (Government Sample).
N: BL[1] = 30; BL = 30; BH[1] = 41; BH = 36; SL[1] = 38; SL = 36; SH[1] = 46; SH = 37. Comparisons—BL[1](46.4) vs. BL(50.8): $t = 2.22$, $p < .05$. BH[1](47.0) vs. BH (52.3): $t = 2.60$, $p < .01$. SL[1](5.0) vs. SL(5.8): $t = 3.79$, $p < .01$. SH[1](5.0) vs. SH (6.1): $t = 4.57$, $p < .01$.

the probability attitude groups for the high importance managers when the ratings of effort are considered (1.0 in private and 1.1 in government) and a smaller difference in all the other comparisons. Thus, when considered together, the data consistently tend to indicate that the strongest relationships between the job behavior ratings and the index of the probability that pay depends upon performance comes when the ratings of effort are considered for the managers to whom pay is of high importance.

Hypothesis 4–D stated that attitudes toward the perceived probability that pay depends upon effort will be more closely related to the job behavior measures than will be the perceived probability that pay depends upon quality of job performance. In order to test this hypothesis, we had to look at the relationship among the three items that made up our composite index of the perceived probability that pay depends upon job performance factors (i.e., the factors of effort, performance and productivity) and the actual job behavior measures. Analysis of these data offered no support for Hypothesis 4–D. Each of the three items were about equally strongly related to the job behavior measures. The fact that the data do not support Hypothesis 4–D is not surprising in view of the relatively high correlations among the three items. (Refer to Table 4–1.) Although the analysis of the three items separately leads us to reject Hypothesis 4–D, this analysis did provide some data that offer additional support for several earlier hypotheses. In line with Hypothesis 4–B, each item was more strongly related to the effort measure than to the job performance measure. Further, as predicted by Hypothesis 4–C, the relationship between each item and the job behavior measures was higher for the high than for the low importance group.

Hypothesis 4–E stated that the more an individual sees his pay as a satisfier, the harder he will work to perform his job effectively. Figure 4–7 shows that there is a consistent tendency for high ratings on both effort and quality of job performance to be associated with seeing pay as a satisfier. This is illustrated in the figure by the continuing increase in the height of the four lines as they move from left to right.

Figure 4–8 presents the data from the government sample that are relevant to Hypothesis 4–E. As can be seen, the data are in essential agreement with those presented in Figure 4–7. Two of the four differences between the high and low pay-as-a-satisfier groups are statistically significant, and, in the other two cases, the results are in the expected direction. Further, there is a consistent

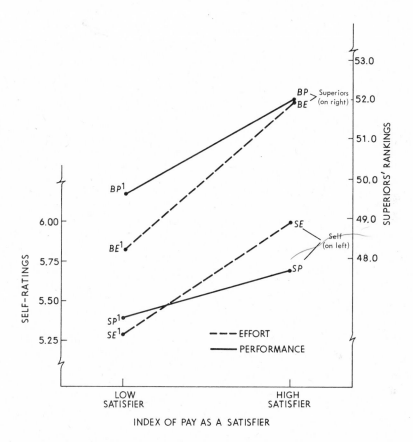

Figure 4–7. Mean self and superiors' ratings of job performance and effort for high and low satisfier groups (Private Industry Sample).

N: $BP^1 = 96$; $BP = 89$; $BE^1 = 91$; $BE = 91$; $SP^1 = 102$; $SP = 102$; $SE^1 = 102$; $SE = 102$. Comparisons—$BP^1(49.6)$ vs. $BP(52.0)$: $t = 1.89$, $p < .05$. $BE^1(48.2)$ vs. $BE(51.9)$: $t = 2.66$, $p < .01$. $SP^1(5.4)$ vs. $SP(5.7)$: $t = 1.77$, $p < .05$. $SE^1(5.3)$ vs. $SE(6.0)$: $t = 4.12$, $p < .01$.

tendency for the high pay-as-a-satisfier group to be rated higher on the job behavior measures than the low group (four out of four cases). Thus, when considered together, the data from both the private and the government samples offer considerable support for Hypothesis 4–E.

Hypothesis 4–F predicted that the managers' attitudes toward the degree to which pay is seen as a satisfier will be more closely related to the amount of effort they put forth on the job than to

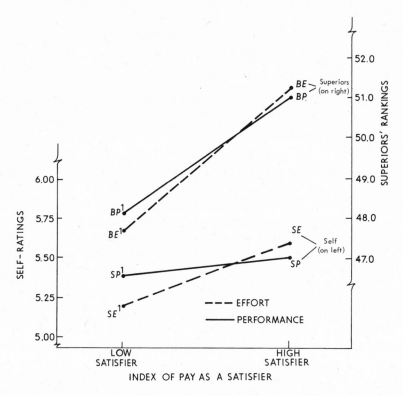

Figure 4–8. Mean self and superiors' ratings of job performance and effort for high and low satisfier groups (Government Sample).

N: $BP^1 = 60$; $BP = 91$; $BE^1 = 60$; $BE = 91$; $SP^1 = 72$; $SP = 91$; $SE^1 = 72$; $SE = 97$. Comparisons—$BP^1(48.1)$ vs. $BP(51.0)$: $t = 1.42$, n.s. $BE^1(47.7)$ vs. $BE(51.2)$: $t = 2.42$, $p < .01$. $SP^1(5.4)$ vs. $SP(5.5)$: $t = .40$, n.s. $SE^1(5.2)$ vs. $SE (5.6)$: $t = 2.60$, $p < .01$.

the quality of their job performance. The data presented in Figures 4–7 and 4–8 are relevant for this hypothesis and appear to offer support for it. For example, in Figure 4–7 the difference between the high and low pay-as-a-satisfier groups is larger for the ratings of effort than for the ratings of quality of performance. This finding holds for both the self and the superiors' rankings and is illustrated in the figure by the steeper slopes of the lines (dotted) representing the ratings of effort.

The data presented in Figure 4–8 for the government sample are also in agreement with the hypothesis. Again the figure shows a steeper line for the ratings on effort than for the ratings of quality of job performance, indicating a stronger relationship

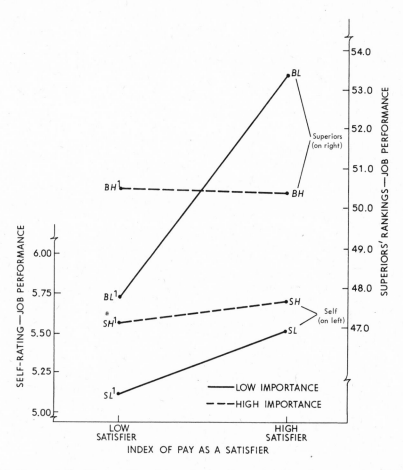

Figure 4–9. Mean self and superiors' ratings of job performance for high and low pay-as-a-satisfier groups with two levels of pay importance (Private Industry Sample).

N: $BL^1 = 40$; $BL = 52$; $BH^1 = 56$; $BH = 55$; $SL^1 = 43$; $SL = 57$; $SH^1 = 59$; $SH = 62$. Comparisons—$BL^1(47.9)$ vs. $BL(53.3)$: $t = 3.04$, $p < .01$. $BH^1(50.5)$ vs. $BH(50.4)$: $t = .28$, n.s. $SL^1(5.1)$ vs. $SL(5.5)$: $t = 2.48$, $p < .01$. $SH^1(5.6)$ vs $SH(5.7)$: $t = .76$, n.s.

exists for the ratings on effort than for the ratings on quality of job performance. It is also shown in Figure 4–8 that the differences between the high and low pay-as-a-satisfier groups are not significant on the two ratings of job performance but are significant on the ratings of effort. Thus the data support the general conclusion that attitudes toward the degree to which pay is seen as a satisfier are more closely related to the amount of effort put forth than to the quality of job performance.

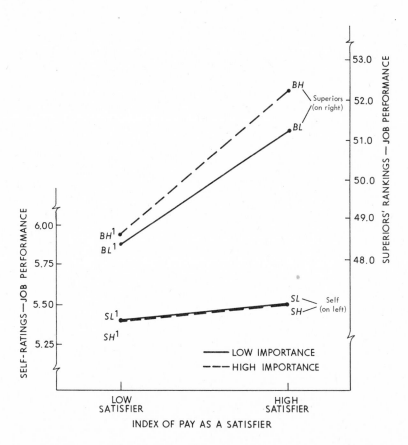

Figure 4–10. Mean self and superiors' ratings of job performance for high and low pay-as-a-satisfier groups with two levels of pay importance. (Government Sample).

N: BL[1] = 35; BL = 29; BH[1] = 37; BH = 41; SL[1] = 43; SL = 32; SH[1] = 31; SH = 43. Comparisons—BL[1](48.4) vs. BL(51.2): $t = 1.43$, n.s. BH[1] (48.6) vs. BH(52.2): $t = 1.87$, $p < .05$. SL[1](5.4) vs. SL(5.5): $t = .48$, n.s. SH[1] (5.4) vs. SH(5.5): $t = .39$, n.s.

Hypothesis 4–G predicted that the relationship between an individual's attitudes toward the degree to which pay is seen as a satisfier and his effort directed to performing effectively will be stronger for those managers who say their pay is important to them than for those who say it is unimportant. Figures 4–9, 4–10, 4–11 and 4–12 present the data relevant to this hypothesis. The data offer no support for the hypothesis. There is no consistent tendency for the relationship between the index of pay as a satis-

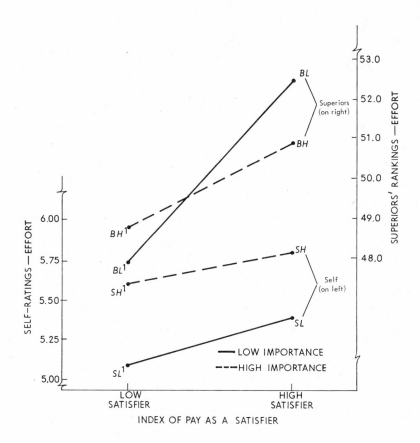

Figure 4–11. Mean self and superiors' ratings of effort for high and low pay-as-a-satisfier groups with two levels of pay importance (Private Industry Sample).

N: BL[1] = 40; BL = 52; BH[1] = 57; BH = 57; SL[1] = 43; SL = 57; SH[1] = 59; SH = 62. Comparisons—BL[1](47.9) vs. BL(52.5): $t = 2.49$, $p < .01$. BH[1](48.7) vs. BH(50.9): $t = 1.32$, n.s. SL[1](5.1) vs. SL(5.4): $t = 1.53$, n.s. SH[1](5.6) vs. SH (5.8): $t = .92$, n.s.

fier and the job behavior measures of effort and performance to be
stronger for the high importance groups than for the low importance groups.

For example, in Figure 4–9 (p. 83), for the superiors' rankings

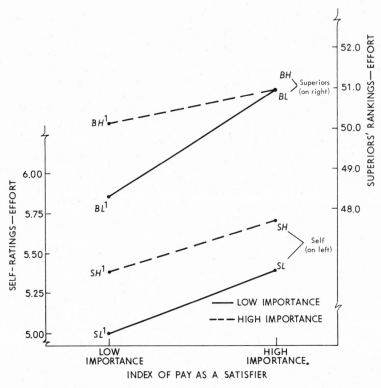

Figure 4–12. Mean self and superiors' ratings of effort for high and low
pay-as-a-satisfier groups with two levels of pay importance (Government
Sample).

N: $BL^1 = 35$; $BL = 29$; $BH^1 = 37$; $BH = 41$; $SL^1 = 43$; $SL = 32$; $SH^1 = 43$;
$SH = 44$. Comparisons—$BL^1(48.3)$ vs. $BL(50.9)$: $t = 1.21$; n.s. $BH^1(50.1)$ vs.
$BH(50.9)$: $t = .54$, n.s. $SL^1(5.0)$ vs. $SL(5.4)$: $t = 1.53$, n.s. $SH^1(5.4)$ vs. SH
(5.7): $t = 1.04$, n.s.

of performance, there is a stronger relationship between attitudes
toward pay as a satisfier and performance for the low importance
group (solid line) than for the high importance group (dotted
line). A similar trend appears for the self-ratings on performance
presented in Figure 4–9. The data presented in Figure 4–10 (p.
84) show that for the superiors' rankings the hypothesis is sup-

ported, but for the self-ratings it is not. Similarly, inconsistent results appear in Figures 4–11 and 4–12. Thus, it appears that on the basis of the data, Hypothesis 4–G must be rejected.

DISCUSSION AND IMPLICATIONS OF THE FINDINGS

Attitudes toward How Pay Is Determined

The results of the present study offer strong support for that part of the model which predicted that seeing a high probability that significant rewards depend upon job performance factors will lead to effort being directed toward performing effectively. The results clearly showed that those managers who saw their pay as dependent upon their job performance were the most effective and highly motivated managers. This same finding appeared in both the self and the superiors' evaluations of performance. Although the present study established empirically the effects of seeing one reward—in this case, pay—as depending upon good job performance, it does seem reasonable that seeing other significant rewards as being contingent upon job performance would have, as predicted by the model, the same relationship to job performance factors. This was the finding of Georgopoulos *et al.* in their study that looked at attitudes toward promotion, pay, and getting along in the work group. It is particularly significant that the Georgopoulos *et al.* study obtained results similar to ours, since theirs was done among workers rather than managers, thus extending the finding to a different sample and situation. This, taken together with the fact that in the present study the same results were found in two rather broad and diverse management samples, indicates strongly that the model's prediction that seeing significant rewards as tied to good performance will lead to a strong attempt to perform effectively may have general validity.

A significant part of the prediction of our model about the kinds of attitudes that lead managers to devote effort to effective job performance was that the value of pay does not combine in an additive form with expectancy to determine performance. Because of the belief that it combines multiplicatively, the hypothesis was derived that the relationship between probability attitudes and effort would be stronger for those managers who attach high reward value to pay than for those who attach to it low reward value. The results of the study generally tend to support this part of the model. A consistent tendency did appear in both samples for the relationship to be stronger in the high than in the low importance groups. However, it should be pointed out that in the low importance groups, some relationship between the probability attitudes and the behavior measures was found. This undoubtedly came about because, even for the low importance group, pay was of greater than zero importance. Because of this, it was impossible to test directly whether a multiplicative relationship exists, since, ideally, a situation in which importance can be varied from zero upward is needed. However, it does seem possible to conclude from the results of the present study that importance has a significant moderating effect on the relationship between expectancy attitudes and job performance.

The prediction that attitudes toward the likelihood that effort influences pay would be more closely related to the job behavior measures than would the attitudes toward the likelihood that performance influences pay was not supported by the data. Apparently, among the managers in our study, there was little tendency to distinguish between the concepts of pay being tied to performance and that of pay being tied to effort. It is, of course, possible that for the managers in these organizations this might not have been a crucial distinction because there was no difficulty converting effort into performance. Indeed, this would seem to make sense in terms of the jobs these managers had. This is, of course, an inference and cannot be supported by the data we collected. Unfortunately, we did not directly ask the managers to estimate the probability that effort on their part would result in good performance. If it were found in future studies that this probability was always close to 1.0, then indeed it could be dropped from the model. However, at this point, we still feel that it may be relevant in many situations. Further, we feel that its characteristics, and how, if at all, it combines with the pay-performance probability to determine job behavior are prime topics for future research.

It should be pointed out that the evidence from the present study does not establish that the attitudes toward how pay is determined in part caused a manager's job performance. What the data do show is that there is a relationship between the attitudes and the performance. The model predicts that the reason for this relationship is that the attitudes affect the performance, but the data cannot directly test this aspect of the model. It is true that the assumption of a causal relationship gives the most parsimonious and face-valid explanation of the several relationships found. In particular, a causal interpretation easily handles, and in fact predicts, the finding of a closer relationship between the attitudes and effort than between the attitudes and job performance. Further, a causal interpretation correctly predicts that importance will serve as a moderator of the relationship between the attitudes and the performance measures.

Alternative explanations of the finding that expectancy attitudes are related to the job performance measures would be that the job performance caused the attitudes or that a third variable caused both the attitudes and the job performance. It is possible to reason from dissonance theory (Festinger, 1957) that job performance might have the power to cause probability attitudes. The reasoning would be that a manager tries to justify his high performance to himself by saying that it will result in higher pay. Another way of stating this is that a high producer might need to feel that he is getting some reward for his work and, thus, he says his pay is a reward for his performance. However, it is not clear how this explanation can handle the finding that the attitudes were more strongly related to effort than to job performance. In addition, it is not clear how such an explanation would handle the finding that importance functions as a moderator variable. Thus, barring further evidence to the contrary, it does not seem reasonable at this time to assume that the job performance caused the expectancy attitudes.

There are a number of possible third variables that might have caused the relationships found, but the one that suggests itself first is salary. The amount of salary received presumably might have the power to cause both the attitudes and the performance. Or, salary could be caused by the performance which, in turn, could cause the attitudes. The good performer who gets high pay may feel the need to believe it is based upon his merit, whereas the poor performer who gets low pay may blame the system and say that merit is not rewarded in his organization. However, since in all the organizations studied, but particularly in the govern-ment organizations, the amount of pay received was not strongly related to the performance measures, this possible explanation would not appear to hold up. Other possible third variables, such as personality traits or situational characteristics, cannot be ruled out completely until evidence from adequately controlled ex-periments exists. However, it does appear that the most reasonable conclusion at this stage is that expectancy attitudes and percep-tions can influence job performance factors.

Attitudes toward Pay as a Satisfier

The evidence from the present study points to a consistent, although moderate, relationship between the degree to which pay is seen as a satisfier and the motivation to perform a job effectively. Positive relationships were found in both samples and when both the self and superiors' evaluations were used. Thus, the results are in agreement with the study of Herzberg *et al.* (1959) who found that higher self-ratings of job performance will result when man-agers see their pay as a satisfier. This finding is also in agreement with our model since, as was pointed out, seeing pay as a satisfier seems to mean that significant rewards are seen as being dependent upon good job performance. Thus, the conclusion that seeing pay as a satisfier is associated with high job performance is congruent with both our model and the Herzberg theory.

Both our model and the Herzberg theory imply that attitudes toward pay as a satisfier lead to changes in the motivation to per-form effectively, but as was pointed out previously, the type of data gathered in the present study does not allow us to test for causal relationships between the attitudes and performance. Thus, it is somewhat risky to assume that because the attitudes and the performance are related, the attitudes caused the performance. However, in this case, it seems reasonable to assume that the perception of pay as a satisfier may have led to the job perfor-mance. Such an interpretation makes possible the easy explanation of the finding that these attitudes are more highly related to effort than to quality of job performance. In addition, there is good evidence for believing that when an individual sees that an activity leads to the satisfaction of his needs, the perception of this relationship will cause him to persist in that activity.

Alternative explanations, either that the job performance caused the attitudes or that a third variable caused both, cannot easily account for the stronger relationships with effort than with quality of performance. The third variable that seems most likely to be able to cause both the attitudes and the job performance would be the amount of salary the managers receive and the kind of raises they have received. However, since actual pay is not highly correlated with either the job performance measures or the attitudes, it is unlikely that this is the third variable. Thus, it is reasonable to conclude that the managers' perceptions of their pay as a satisfier does bear a causal relationship to their job performance.

Hypothesis 4–G predicted that the importance of pay as a satisfier would operate as a moderator of the relationship between the degree to which pay is seen as a satisfier, and the measures of job performance. The data offered no support for this hypothesis. Two explanations appear to exist for the failure of this hypothesis to be supported by the data. It may be that a measure of the importance of pay is different from a measure of the importance of pay as a satisfier. This would mean that seeing pay as a satisfier means more than just seeing pay as related to performance. It may mean that other rewards are seen to be tied to pay also, and that an adequate importance measure must be a measure of the importance of all these rewards. Some support for this interpretation comes from the low correlation (average $r = .28$) between the index of pay as a satisfier and the index of probability that pay depends upon job performance. This would seem to indicate that these two measures are tapping somewhat different areas and indicate that the same importance measure cannot function for both.

A second reason for the lack of support for this hypothesis may be that for pay to be seen as a satisfier, it must be important. If this is true, then using importance as a moderator would have only the effect of separating individuals on the degree to which they see pay as a satisfier. Thus, it is obvious that before an adequate measure of the importance of pay as a satisfier can be developed, further understanding is needed of what it means, in terms of the various psychological needs, for pay to be seen as a satisfier.

Effort and Job Performance

The model predicted that attitudes which are reflections of an individual's desire to perform will be more closely related to the ratings of effort than to the ratings of quality of job performance. The results for both attitudes toward how pay is determined and attitudes toward pay as a satisfier supported this part of the model. Because of the nature of the data it was impossible to test whether a multiplicative relationship exists among the determinants of performance, but the data do show that effort is more closely related to the attitudes, as would be necessary if a multiplicative relationship exists.

One significant implication of the relationship between the attitudes and the ratings on effort is that if researchers are to find a relationship between attitudes that are measures of motivation and behavior, they probably should stop looking at just a simple criterion of productivity or quality of job performance. It appears that since both ability and correctness of role perceptions influence performance along with effort, attitudes can never be very highly related to simple measures of quality of job performance. Thus, future studies should consider using a more direct measure of an individual's desire to perform well, or attempt to separate the effects of ability and role perceptions from those of effort, when they are attempting to understand the impact of attitudes on performance.

Pay as an Incentive

One of the central concerns of this chapter has been with the importance of pay as an incentive in the job situation. The finding that attitudes about pay are related to job performance provides information on *when* pay can be expected to function as an incentive. Specifically, it appears reasonable to conclude that pay can be an incentive for better job performance when it is important to the individual and when it is seen as being tied to job performance. There is some evidence that organization policies can influence both of these perceptions.

Recently, investigators (i.e., Nealey, 1963; Mahoney, 1964; Jones and Jeffrey, 1964) have found that the value to the employee of the same amount of pay may vary greatly, depending upon how it is divided among various fringe benefits and options. Presumably, this comes about because certain benefits better fit the motive patterns of employees and are, therefore, valued more than are other benefits. This seems to occur despite the fact that the benefits may cost the company exactly the same amount of money. Other data suggest that because different employees have different motives, large individual differences appear in the degree to which individuals value various options. Nealey (1963), for example, found that unmarried workers value time off highly, while married workers do not. Clearly, these two groups have different motives operating, and, as a result, time off has different meanings to them.

The implications of the pay preference research are rather interesting as far as practices in the compensation area are concerned. Perhaps the most important one is that if organizations are to maximize the perceived value of the financial incentives they offer, then a "cafeteria" style wage plan is needed. A cafeteria compensation plan would allow every employee to divide his compensation dollars among the options he values most without adding to the total compensation costs of the company. Such a plan would appear to be potentially most effective at the management level. At this level there are fewer problems with union contracts and other agreements that might limit the organization's freedom. In addition, it makes more sense to offer alternative ways of determining pay to managers, since such things as stock options and profit-sharing plans are feasible. The evidence, then, seems to suggest that one way to increase the importance of pay without increasing the actual amount of money spent is to relate the form of compensation more directly to the motives of the managers by using a cafeteria style wage plan.

It has been pointed out previously that most organizations practice secrecy with respect to management compensation and that it may have negative effects in terms of satisfaction with pay (Lawler, 1965–a, 1965–b, 1967–b). It is also possible that secrecy may decrease the importance managers attach to the amount of their pay. Admittedly, there is little data either to support or reject this argument, but it would seem to agree with the view that pay gains its value from its association with the satisfaction of status, recognition, and achievement needs. By keeping pay secret, organizations are making it less directly instrumental for the satisfaction of these needs. After all, the needs for recognition and status are inherently public in nature, and, if salary is truly kept secret, then it is difficult to see how salary can be effectively related to them. Promotion stands today as one of the major incentives stimulating managerial performance. Because of its very public nature, it sensitizes managers' needs for recognition and status. Were pay to be public, it, like promotion, might be able to satisfy a broad range of important needs.

At this point, we need considerable research on the impact of making pay public before we will have a good idea of its significance. However, it does seem likely that one area which would be affected is the manager's view of how important the amount of his pay is to him.

So far we have considered several factors that may influence the importance and value of pay as a reward where the amount of pay remains the same. It is obvious that one other way to increase the importance of a particular financial reward or salary increase is to increase the absolute amount of money given. But the relationship may not be a simple linear one between the value of the raise to the individual and the amount of money given. It has long been known that for a person making $1,000 a month a $10 raise will have much less value than it will for a person making $200 a month. Obviously, salary increases, in order to be meaningful to managers at all salary levels, need to be based upon some proportion of the manager's present salary. Most organizations are aware of this and use a percentage figure for computing raises, but many seem to use a figure that is too small. Unfortunately, there is not enough research evidence available upon which to base a definite statement about the amount of the percentage raise that must be given if it is to be meaningful.

Although the present study was not designed to determine what type of pay programs lead to the perception that pay is based upon performance, the differences between the private and government samples on the index of the perceived probability that pay is dependent on performance are interesting in this regard. As was pointed out, the private organizations had pay plans that attempted to tie pay more closely to job performance than did the pay plans of the government organizations. From a comparison between the two samples on the degree to which pay was seen to be tied to performance, it is clear that the private managers actually did see their pay as more closely tied to their performance.[6] The implication of this difference is obvious. Organizations can do something to foster the belief among their employees that their pay is based upon their performance. Future research will undoubtedly investigate the relative effectiveness of different pay plans in this respect, but even at the present time there appear to be some recommendations that can be made concerning how to encourage the belief that pay depends upon job performance.

We have already discussed some of the implications of secrecy about management compensation, but what we have not pointed out is that it may have considerable impact upon managers' perceptions of how their pay is determined. With secrecy existent in an organization, a situation is created in which it is very difficult for a manager to know how his pay compares with other managers' pay in the organization. This, of course, means that he has no objective basis against which to test his beliefs concerning the question of who gets paid well in the organization. Consequently, he has little information upon which to base his estimate of what kind of behavior leads to financial success in the organization. Also, he gets little feedback about how well he is performing in relation to others in the organization and as a result does not know how to adjust his performance in order to bring it more in line with what is acceptable to the organization. He is forced to fall back upon his own estimate of what others make in order to evaluate his performance and, as Lawler (1965–a) has pointed out, these estimates are often wrong. The results of these effects of secrecy hardly seem to be likely to do anything but raise questions in the minds of managers about the validity of the frequently heard statement that "pay and performance are closely related in this organization."

In an attempt to tie pay to performance, stock option plans and bonus or profit-sharing plans are often used. At this point, it seems appropriate to ask: Do these kinds of pay plans really accomplish that purpose? It is very unlikely, for example, that

[6]See Appendix V for this comparison.

stock option plans create the perception among managers that their own job behavior will actually influence their pay, since for this to happen they must feel that they can influence the price of the stock on the stock exchange. There are simply too many factors influencing stock prices for a single manager's effectiveness to be related to them. The same problems appear to exist with many bonus and profit-sharing plans; that is, they often fail to create the perception that individual managerial behavior is directly related to financial outcomes. Unfortunately, profits and other "objective" measures of performance are often almost completely out of the control of the individual manager, no matter what his organizational position may be. In one sense, such plans are rather poor substitutes for an effective performance appraisal system. In removing the control over a manager's economic returns from the immediate job situation, stock option and bonus plans may take the pressure off his superior for making subjective performance appraisals, but this may be done at the cost of destroying the relationship between pay and performance. An obvious truism would seem to be that without an effective performance appraisal system, pay can never be an effective incentive.

Haire *et al.* (1963) have called pay the most important incentive in our society. The results of the present study support the conclusion that it is a major incentive, although they do not offer unequivocal support for the statement that it is the most important incentive. The results do allow us to reject Brown's (1962) view that pay is not an important determinant of job performance. In the course of 50 years, we have moved from a firm belief in the concept of "economic man" to an equally firm belief in "social man" and "self-actualizing man." Research evidence suggests that both these extreme views are fallacious. However, it is not so surprising that both these divergent views have at one time enjoyed wide acceptance. Psychologists interested in individual differences have long known that no matter what model of man is created, it is possible to find someone who fits it. Thus, data exist which support both views.

The answer to the question of whether "social man," "self-actualizing man" or "economic man" represents the best model for organization theorists to follow when they deal with motivation is that none is *the* best. The fact is that man is motivated by social and self-actualization needs as well as by economic needs. What we really have is what Schein (1965) has called "complex man." The best motivational system for "complex man" will always be one that relates to a variety of needs, including economic ones, in order to motivate good job performance. Our model points out that the more the satisfaction of these needs can be tied to effective performance, the higher will be the motivation to perform effectively.

CHAPTER 5

Role Perceptions

The model presented in Chapter 2 indicates that the appropriateness of a manager's role perceptions has an important influence on the quality of his job performance. However, the model does not attempt to specify what the correct role perceptions are likely to be in a given situation. The model merely points out that regardless of an individual's level of effort, if his role perceptions are inappropriate for his job, then good performance is unlikely. Undoubtedly, different jobs, and perhaps even the same job in different organizations, frequently require a manager to have different kinds of role perceptions if he is to be successful. Nevertheless, there is one role perception dimension that frequently has been suggested as being applicable to most management jobs. This dimension is the "inner-other-directed" dimension first mentioned by Riesman (1950).

Evidence that managers' role perceptions on this dimension are consistently related to effective job performance would offer support for our model. Such evidence would serve to illustrate that at least one role perception dimension has a significant influence upon managerial job performance. In order to determine the kinds of relationships that might be expected between job performance and the "inner-other-directed" dimension, let us look briefly at the views of David Riesman and William H. Whyte, Jr., and also at the empirical evidence relevant to this dimension.

THE WRITINGS OF RIESMAN AND WHYTE

Prior to the 1950's it was a part of American folklore that the way to succeed in American business was to follow in the footsteps of great individualists like Henry Ford or John D. Rockefeller. These men were known for their forcefulness and imagination, and they were seldom accused of being tactful or cautious. What did the rising young businessman need in order to accomplish great things? It was generally accepted that, given sufficient ability and motivation, what he needed was to demonstrate the kind of imagination and independence that had characterized the Fords and Rockefellers of an earlier generation. However, with the advent of the 1950's and in particular with the publication of two books—*The Lonely Crowd* by Riesman (1950) and *The Organization Man* by Whyte (1956)—this picture of the qualities that lead to success in American business was seriously questioned. The thrust of both books was that the individualist no longer had a place in middle and lower levels of management in our large corporations. According to Riesman, for example, success is now coming to the "other-directed" person, the individual who is supersensitive to the thinking and desires of other individuals. Because of the heavy emphasis by Whyte and Riesman on the point that the inner- or other-directed dimension is important in determining management effectiveness, the decision was made to collect data relevant to it. Specifically, we decided to look at the relationship between the degree to which managers feel other-directed kinds of behavior are required in their jobs and how successfully they are seen to be performing their jobs. By looking at this relationship it will be possible to determine not only if role perceptions have the kind of relationship to performance that our model predicts, but also to test the validity of Riesman's and Whyte's contentions about the importance of having other-directed role perceptions if one is to be successful in modern organizations.

"This is a book about social character . . . it is about the way in which one kind of social character, which dominated America in the nineteenth century, is gradually being replaced by a social character of a different sort." (Riesman, 1950, p. 1). With this statement Riesman begins the much-discussed book, *The Lonely Crowd*. The social character that is being replaced in Riesman's eyes is the "inner-directed" person. The inner-directed man is one who relies on his own ideas and his own values in determining his behavior; to use Riesman's word for it, he has his own internal "gyroscope." The inner-directed man is being replaced, according to Riesman, by the other-directed man who uses the behavior and thinking of people around him as guides for his own thinking and behavior. According to Riesman, inner-direction is typical of the "old entrepreneurs," while other-direction is becoming the typical characteristic of the "new middle class as exemplified by the bureaucrat and the salaried employee in business." How does one get to the top in business today? According to Riesman, to get to the top in our large organizations one has to learn a "personality-oriented specialty or manipulative skill." Thus, the clear direction of Riesman's argument is that other-directed role perceptions and role behavior are the qualities required for success in business today.

Six years after Riesman's book appeared, Whyte (1956) attacked the business world much more directly in *The Organization Man*. Whyte spoke of the social ethic and of the kind of behavior it requires of one who is to succeed in the large organization. Whyte's thesis fits in easily with Riesman's views. According to Whyte, the modern American firm, especially the large firm, demands a type of conformity and go-along-with-the-crowd behavior. Managers are pictured by Whyte as being rewarded for being noncontroversial, adaptable, and, in short, for not rocking the boat. The "organization man," says Whyte, must sacrifice some of his individuality and creativity if he is to succeed. Although Whyte paints this picture as applying rather generally to American business, he says it appears particularly in large organizations, and particularly in lower and middle management—more than in top management. The similarity between Whyte's and Riesman's arguments is obvious; whether you call him an "organization man" or "other-directed" is inconsequential. For both Whyte and Riesman the adaptable, socially attuned individual is going to succeed in business, while the creative, independent individual is in for trouble.

That the thesis of Whyte and Riesman has had an impact is undeniable. Many have uncritically accepted the validity of their arguments and used them as a basis for criticizing large organizations (Porter, 1964). Almost everyone has come out against conformity. A study by Olmsted (1957), for example, found that most Smith College students considered themselves to be more inner-directed than other students. Recruiters of college graduates for large organizations have probably wished many times that these books weren't devoured so completely by undergraduates. The image of business as a place demanding conformity has reportedly caused many individuals to choose other careers. One of the most successful plays on Broadway in recent years, *How to Succeed in Business without Really Trying,* depicts how the perfect "organization man" gets ahead in business. However, despite the obvious public, as well as academic, interest in the ideas of Whyte and Riesman, only four relevant empirical research studies could be located on this topic.

PREVIOUS RESEARCH

The first study that provides some evidence with respect to the relative success of managers with inner- and other-directed values was done by Fleishman and Peters (1962). They studied middle managers in a large industrial organization—just the situation in which, according to Whyte and Riesman, the other-directed individual should do best. Two kinds of data were collected for each manager. First, he was rated by his superior on the quality of his job performance, and secondly, he took the Gordon (1960) *Survey of Interpersonal Values.* The Gordon instrument has a conformity scale which is designed to measure the degree to which an individual values doing what is socially accepted and proper, following regulations closely, and being a conformist. Fleishman and Peters found a significant tendency ($r = -.44$) for those individuals who scored *low* on conformity to be rated higher on job performance by their superiors than were those managers who scored high on conformity—a finding that appears to be directly contrary to that which would be expected from the writings of Riesman and Whyte. A recent follow-up study by Hay (1964) has replicated this finding, further questioning the validity of Riesman's and Whyte's point.

Roadman (1964) has also done a study that provides some interesting data about the kinds of individuals who succeed in business. He studied 56 middle managers in a large industrial organization. Peer ratings were obtained for each manager on factors such as originality, independence, cooperation with others, and tact. The promotion rates of these managers were observed over the next two years. The results showed that the majority of the promotions went to those managers who were described as being relatively high on originality, independence of thought, aggressiveness, and self-expression, but relatively low on tact and cooperation with others. Thus, the Roadman study is in substantial agreement with those done by Fleishman and Peters in finding that the individuals who appear to be other-directed are not the most successful managers, but are in fact the least successful.

Porter (1964) has approached the questions raised by Riesman and Whyte from a different perspective. Using a sample of almost 2,000 managers from all levels of management and from companies ranging widely in size, he asked managers to rate 10 personality-type traits on the basis of how important they were for success in their management positions. Five of these adjective trait descriptions were considered to be other-directed (e.g., tactful, cooperative), and five were considered to be inner-directed (e.g., imaginative, forceful). Thus, Porter was measuring the individual's perception of the kind of role behavior that leads to success in his managerial position. In contrast to the Roadman study, however, no direct measure of managerial behavior was obtained by Porter. Nevertheless, a reasonably close correspondence between the role perceptions of a manager and his actual role behavior should exist if the manager is motivated to succeed and if he is capable of behaving in the appropriate way. Evidence to support this latter point can be found in a recent study (Lawler and Porter, 1967–a). In this study, each manager was asked to rank the traits both on the basis of how important they are for success and on the basis of how well they describe his behavior. A significant correlation ($r = .61$) was found between the two rankings, supporting the point that role perceptions and role behavior are probably closely related for most managers.

As might have been expected from Whyte's views, Porter found that line managers tended to feel that inner-directed behavior was more important than did staff managers. However, contrary to

expectation, there was a tendency for managers in large organizations to place less emphasis on the other-directed traits than did
those in small organizations. Porter also found that higher level
managers placed more importance on inner-directed behavior
than did lower level managers. One possible explanation for this
finding is that higher level positions actually do require and obtain more inner-directed behavior from their incumbents. Another explanation that also appears to be valid in the light of the
Roadman study is that those managers who tend to see lower level
jobs as demanding inner-directed behavior, and behave accordingly, obtain faster promotions and carry this tendency with them
into their higher level positions. The other-directed role per-
ceivers, on the other hand, may not get promoted as frequently,
and thus the lower levels contain more other-directed types. The
Porter data interpreted in this way, and taken together with the
data from the three other studies, would appear to suggest that
large organizations positively reward, rather than discriminate
against, the inner-directed type.

HYPOTHESES

In the model presented in Chapter 2 it was stressed that correct
role perceptions were a necessary prerequisite for effective job
performance. Using this model, the expectation would be that with
ability and motivation held constant, managers with "correct" role
perceptions will be more effective performers. Since the sample
in the present study was drawn from middle and lower level
managers in large organizations, one possible hypothesis, based
upon the Riesman and Whyte arguments, would be that managers
with other-directed role perceptions will be rated more highly by
their superiors. However, such a hypothesis does not appear to be
tenable in the light of the research evidence that exists. The evidence (as cited above) shows that even in large industrial
organizations inner-directed, rather than other-directed, behavior
is rewarded. Granted, part of this evidence was gathered for behavior rather than for role perceptions; but as has been pointed
out, role perceptions are assumed to form the basis for role behavior and thus there should be a substantial amount of con-
gruence between them. Therefore, it is expected that the correct

role perceptions in our sample will be in the direction of inner-directed behavior; this leads us to our first hypothesis.

Hypothesis 5–A. The more managers see their jobs as demanding inner-directed behavior, the higher they will be rated on quality of job performance.

Since data were obtained for each manager from his superior on the amount of effort put forth, it is also possible to state a second hypothesis. It was suggested in our discussion of the model that a multiplicative relationship may exist between effort, ability, and role perceptions. The implication is that if any of the three determinants of performance is low, the variance in the other two will have little relationship to performance. In terms of our present study, this allows us to state our second hypothesis.

Hypothesis 5–B. The relationship between role perceptions and performance will be greater for those managers who are rated high on effort than it will be for those managers who are rated low on effort.

ATTITUDE MEASURES OBTAINED

The role perceptions of the managers were measured by asking them to rank 12 personality-type traits.[1] The instructions were (in part) as follows:

The purpose of (this part of) the questionnaire is to obtain a picture of the traits you believe are most necessary for success in *your present management position.*

Below is a list of twelve traits arranged randomly. Rank these twelve traits from 1 to 12 in order of their importance for success in your present management position.

Two of the 12 traits included in the list were camouflage items put there to disguise the dimension being studied. When the data were analyzed, these two items—intelligence and efficiency—were dropped from the analysis and the traits reranked from 1 to 10 with the remaining traits being appropriately elevated in rank as replacements for those that had been removed. Although the respondents were asked to assign the rank 1 to the most important

[1]This part of the follow-up questionnaire is identical to that used by Porter and Henry (1964) in their previous study, and a complete copy of it can be found in Appendix II.

trait, in the data analysis this order was reversed, and the most important trait was given a score of 9. Thus, in Tables 5–1 and 5–2, high numbers mean "more important," with 9 being maximum in importance and 0 being minimum in importance.

In the questionnaire, the 12 traits were presented in random order. Because of the use of the two dummy traits as well as the random order of the other traits, it is unlikely that very many, if any, managers recognized the dimension being considered. This is important because Whyte suggests that the "organization man" does not want to be seen as one. The 10 relevant traits are listed below in the two theoretical clusters used as a basis for the analysis of the results:

Inner-Directed Cluster	*Other-Directed Cluster*
Forceful	Cooperative
Imaginative	Adaptable
Independent	Cautious
Self-confident	Agreeable
Decisive	Tactful

Although the trait clusters identified as inner- and other-directed were created on a purely theoretical basis, using the descriptions of Riesman and Whyte, Porter (1964) did find a tendency for the traits in each cluster to move together. For example, when different management levels were compared, four out of five of the inner-directed traits showed clear trends in the same direction. This provides some evidence that these clusters have empirical as well as theoretical validity.[2]

In the present study, cluster scores were computed for each individual by summing his ranks for the five relevant traits. Thus, a high score on a given dimension (e.g., the inner-directed dimension) means that the five traits comprising that dimension were all rated as relatively important. It is obvious that since ranks were used, a high score on one of the two dimensions necessarily means a low score on the other.

For the purpose of the data analysis, the data for the lower and middle levels of management were analyzed separately. This kind

---

[2]Intercorrelations were not computed for the present sample because the data were in the form of ranks and thus not completely conducive to this kind of analysis.

of breakdown, rather than the government–private industry breakdown used for the pay data, seemed more appropriate for these data, since the previous study by Porter had shown that management level has an impact on role perceptions. Dividing the sample into two management levels also makes it possible to determine if management level differences exist in the present sample. Furthermore, this breakdown makes it possible to test our hypotheses in two independent samples.

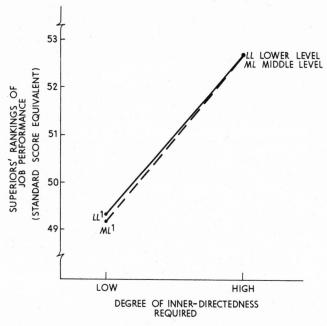

Figure 5–1.   Mean superiors' rankings of job performance for high and low inner-directed groups at two levels of management.

N: LL[1] = 68; LL = 64; ML[1] = 63; ML = 52. Comparisons—LL[1](49.3) vs. LL (52.7): $t = 2.18$, $p < .05$. ML[1](49.2) vs. ML(52.7): $t = 1.65$, $p < .05$.

TESTS OF THE HYPOTHESES

Hypothesis 5–A predicted that managers who see their jobs as requiring high amounts of inner-directed behavior will be rated as better performers than managers who see their jobs as demanding relatively less inner-directed behavior. Figure 5–1 presents the data from the superiors' rankings of quality of performance that are relevant to Hypothesis 5–A. As can be seen, there is a clear trend for those managers in both middle and lower management who have high inner-directed scores to be rated as better performers than those managers who have low inner-directed scores. At both management levels the difference between the high and low inner-directed groups is statistically significant.

Table 5–1 presents the mean ranking for each trait by managers rated in the top third and in the bottom third on job perfor-

TABLE 5–1

Mean Rankings of Traits for the High and Low Job
Performance Groups as Determined by Superiors' Rankings

Inner-Directed Traits	Middle Level Managers		Lower Level Managers	
	Low Performers (N=57)	High Performers (N=57)	Low Performers (N=69)	High Performers (N=78)
Forceful	3.3	3.8	2.9	3.0
Imaginative	5.4	6.1	4.6	5.1
Independent	1.6	2.0	2.0	1.7
Self-confident	6.1	5.5	5.7	6.3
Decisive	5.4	6.1	4.5	5.4
	Σ=21.8	Σ=23.5	Σ=19.7	Σ=21.5
Other-Directed Traits				
Cooperative	6.2	5.9	7.2	6.8
Adaptable	6.1	5.8	5.7	5.6
Cautious	1.6	1.6	2.8	2.6
Agreeable	3.4	2.9	4.7	3.6
Tactful	5.9	5.4	4.5	5.4
	Σ=23.2	Σ=21.6	Σ=25.2	Σ=23.5

mance by their superiors. The results for both levels generally fit the hypothesis. At both levels four out of the five inner-directed traits are ranked as more important by the high performance group, and at both levels four out of the five other-directed traits are ranked as more important by the low performance group. Thus, the evidence from the superiors' evaluations of performance is congruent with Hypothesis 5–A which predicted the high inner-directed managers would be considered the best performers.

Figure 5–2 presents the data from the self-ratings of job performance that are relevant to Hypothesis 5–A. As can be seen,

there is a significant trend for both lower level managers
($p < .01$) and middle level managers ($p < .05$) who have high
inner-directed cluster scores to rate themselves higher on job performance than do those managers who have low inner-directed
cluster scores.

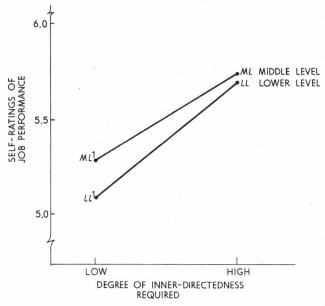

Figure 5–2. Mean self-ratings of job performance for high and low inner-
directed groups at two levels of management.

    N: $LL^1 = 59$; $LL = 47$; $ML^1 = 56$; $ML = 47$.   Comparisons—$LL^1(5.1)$ vs.
$LL(5.7)$: $t = 2.63$, $p < .01$. $ML^1(5.3)$ vs. $ML(5.8)$: $t = 1.73$, $p < .05$.

Table 5–2 presents the mean ranking for each trait by high and
low self-rated performance groups. The results for the lower level
managers clearly support the hypothesis. Three out of five inner-
directed traits are rated as more important by the high rated managers and all five of the other-directed traits are rated as more
important by the low rated performers. The results for the middle level managers, however, fail to offer support for the hypothesis as no consistent differences appeared between the high and
low rated managers. Other than this one exception, however, the
evidence from the self-ratings supports Hypothesis 5–A. When
taken together with the data from the superiors' ratings, the over-

all picture of the data is one that strongly confirms the hypothesis. Four out of the four relationships are significant in the predicted direction, and there is a general tendency for the individual inner-directed traits to be associated in the expected direction with the performance measures. The data for individual trait rankings that appear in Tables 5–1 and 5–2 also show that there is a consistent tendency for the inner-directed traits to be ranked as more important by the middle level managers than by the lower level managers. This finding is congruent with Porter's (1964; Porter and Henry, 1965) previous work which found the same result in a sample of 1900 managers that included all levels of management.

TABLE 5–2

Mean Rankings of Traits by the High and Low
Self-Rated Groups on Quality of Job Performance

	Middle Level Managers		Lower Level Managers	
Inner-Directed Traits	Low Performers (N=37)	High Performers (N=32)	Low Performers (N=37)	High Performers (N=39)
Forceful 4.0		3.5	3.7	3.1
Imaginative 5.2		5.9	3.5	5.3
Independent 1.7		2.2	1.2	2.0
Self-confident 6.0		5.6	6.2	6.7
Decisive 6.5		6.3	5.0	4.9
	Σ=23.4	Σ=23.5	Σ=19.6	Σ=22.0
Other-Directed Traits				
Cooperative 5.3		5.7	6.8	6.7
Adaptable 6.3		5.0	5.9	5.4
Cautious 1.5		1.7	2.7	2.4
Agreeable 2.5		3.2	4.5	3.8
Tactful 5.9		5.9	5.6	4.8
	Σ=21.5	Σ=21.4	Σ=25.5	Σ=23.1

Hypothesis 5–B predicted that the relationship between role perceptions and performance would be stronger for high effort managers than for low effort managers. In order to test this hypothesis, the managers at each level were first divided into two groups on the basis of how much effort their superiors said they put forth on the job; thus, high and low effort groups were ob-

tained at each management level. Within the two effort groups the managers again were divided in half, this time on the basis of their inner-directed cluster scores; thus, for each effort level, high and low inner-directed managers were obtained. Figures 5–3 and 5–4 present the mean superiors' ratings of performance for each of the four groups obtained at each management level. Figure

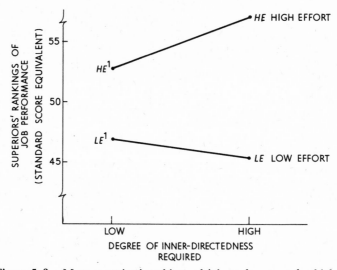

Figure 5–3. Mean superiors' rankings of job performance for high and low inner-directed groups with two levels of effort (middle level managers).

N: $LE^1 = 38$; $LE = 41$; $HE^1 = 42$; $HE = 45$. Comparisons—$LE^1(46.9)$ vs. LE (45.4): $t = .31$, n.s. $HE^1(52.8)$ vs. $HE(57.1)$: $t = 2.76$, $p < .01$.

5–3 shows that at the middle management level there is a significant tendency for the high effort managers to be more highly rated by their superiors if they are in the high, rather than in the low, inner-directed group. This figure also shows that for low effort managers there is no significant performance difference between the high and low inner-directed managers.[3] Thus, the results for the middle level managers are congruent with Hypothesis 5–B.

Figure 5–4 presents the data from the lower level managers that

[3] A two-by-two analysis of variance found a significant ($p < .05$) interaction effect between effort and role perceptions, which adds further support to the hypothesis.

are relevant to Hypothesis 5–B. At this level, the performance difference between the high and low inner-directed managers is significant $(p < .05)$ in both the high and low effort groups. This finding is not congruent with Hypothesis 5–B, since it was expected that an insignificant (or, at least, a less significant) relationship would exist in the low effort group.

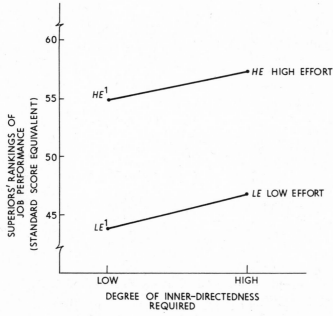

Figure 5–4. Mean superiors' rankings of job performance for high and low inner-directed groups with two levels of effort (lower level managers).
N : LE¹ $= 57$; LE $= 53$; HE¹ $= 57$; HE $= 53$. Comparisons—LE¹(43.7) vs. LE(46.3) : $t = 2.05$, $p < .05$. HE¹(55.0) vs. HE(57.4) : $t = 1.67$, $p < .05$.

Figures 5–5 and 5–6 present the mean self-rating performance scores for the groups considered in Figures 5–3 and 5–4. As in the case of the superiors' ratings, it was expected from Hypothesis 5–B that a stronger relationship between the inner-other-directed dimension and performance would be obtained in the high effort group than in the low effort group. As can be seen, the results for both management levels are congruent with this expectation. At the middle management levels the performance difference between the high and low inner-directed groups is significant

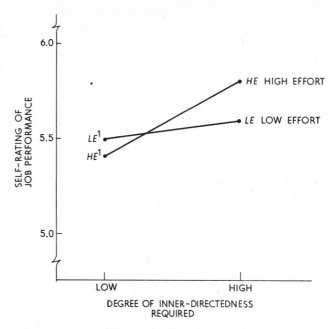

Figure 5–5. Mean self-ratings of job performance for high and low inner-directed groups with two levels of effort (middle level managers).

N: $\text{LE}^1 = 38$; $\text{LE} = 38$; $\text{HE}^1 = 36$; $\text{HE} = 42$. Comparisons—$\text{LE}^1(5.5)$ vs. LE (5.6): $t = .48$, n.s. $\text{HE}^1(5.4)$ vs. HE(5.8): $t = 1.91$, $p < .05$.

($p < .05$) for the high effort managers, and at the lower level it approaches significance ($p < .10$), while at neither level is there any relationship for the low effort managers.[4] This finding, taken together with that obtained from the superiors' ratings, offers tentative support for Hypothesis 5–B. In three out of the four situations viewed (self-ratings, middle and lower level, and superiors' rankings, middle level), the expected relationship was found.[5]

It is important to note in Figures 5–3, 5–4, 5–5, and 5–6 that

---

[4]Interaction effect is significant for middle level managers but is insignificant at the lower level.

[5]It may be noted in Figures 5–5 and 5–6 that the low inner-directed managers tend to rate themselves as better performers when they are in the low rather than in the high effort group. This tendency, however, is not statistically significant and merely reflects the fact that the self-ratings on performance are not related to the superiors' ratings on effort.

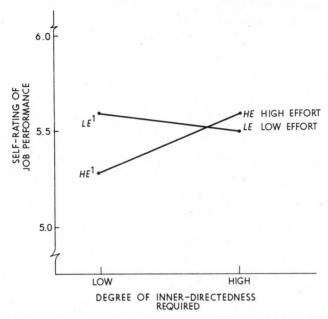

Figure 5–6. Mean self-ratings of job performance for high and low inner-directed groups with two levels of effort (lower level managers).
N: LE[1] = 46; LE = 49; HE[1] = 50; HE = 48. Comparisons—LE[1](5.6) vs. LE (5.5): $t = .30$, n.s. HE[1](5.3) vs. HE(5.6): $t = 1.30$, n.s.

the relationship between performance and the inner-directed dimension held even when the effect of effort was held constant. That is, even where all managers were seen as high in effort by their superiors, some were seen as better performers than were others. This emphasizes the point that the performance differences illustrated by Figures 5–1 and 5–2 between the high and low inner-directed groups is due not to motivational or effort differences but to differences in how appropriately the energy is applied to the job. One possibility is that a simple ability or experience factor, rather than the role perception factor, accounted for the finding that high inner-directed managers appear to convert their motivation into performance more effectively than do low inner-directed managers. In order to test this possibility, comparisons were made between high inner- and low inner-directed managers on the measures of experience and ability that were obtained.

However, no significant differences were found on education level, seniority, or experience that indicated differences in these factors co-varied with inner-other-directedness in a way that could explain the relationship between performance and inner-directedness.

DISCUSSION AND IMPLICATIONS OF THE FINDINGS

The data on role perceptions appear to form a good basis upon which to answer the issues raised at the beginning of this chapter. First, the evidence seems to suggest that, as predicted by our model, role perceptions can have an influence on job performance. Secondly, the evidence does not support Riesman's and Whyte's views about the place of the other-directed man in American management.

The results, as pointed out above, indicate that the role perception dimension has a significant moderating effect on the quality of managerial job performance. Specifically, the results show that those managers who see their jobs as demanding considerable inner-directed behavior are more effective in performing their jobs than are those managers who see their jobs as demanding relatively less inner-directed behavior. This is in line with our model which specifies that role perceptions are an important variable in determining how a manager will convert his effort into actual job performance. Thus, the expectation based upon the model was that role perceptions and job performance would be related. Since the present study is not of an experimental nature, it is impossible to determine with certainty whether or not the relationship found between role perceptions and performance came about because, as the model predicted, role perceptions moderate the relationship between effort and performance. Strictly speaking, all that our data prove is that role perceptions and performance are related.

We have already pointed out that there are a number of conditions that can produce a correlation between two variables. The question in the present section of our study is, which of these factors led to the observed relationship between role perceptions and performance? Did the role perceptions lead to the behavior, did the behavior lead to the role perceptions, or did some third variable cause both of them?

Causal Basis for the Findings

In the case of the present data, it seemed that motivation and ability factors were the third variables that were most likely to be capable of causing the role perceptions and job performance to vary together. However, the results show that even with effort held constant, the relationship between role perceptions and performance exists, allowing us to eliminate motivation as a possible third variable causing the relationship. It was also found that the measures of ability that were available did not relate to the role perception data in such a way as to be a third possible causal variable. Although the available measures of ability were crude, it does seem that if ability did have a significant relationship to the role perception measure, some relationship would have appeared even with these measures. Thus, the two most likely third variables, motivation and ability, probably can be discounted as determinants of the relationship found between role perceptions and performance, making it more likely that a causal relationship exists between the two.

The question of whether the role perception differences caused the performance differences or the performance differences may have caused the role perception differences cannot be answered directly from the present data. However, on logical grounds it is hard to see how the differences in performance might cause the role perception differences found among the managers. It is particularly hard to see why performance would have a causal effect on role perceptions for high effort managers but not for low effort managers, and as the results indicate, just such an interactive relationship appears to exist. On the other hand, it is easy to imagine that a manager's feelings about whether he should be cautious or forceful will have a direct impact on how he carries out any aspect of his job and consequently on how adequately he is seen as performing his job. Similarly, the interactive relationship between effort and role perceptions is easily explained and, in fact, is predicted if it is assumed that the role perception differences lead to the performance differences. In summary, the data are suggestive of the fact that, as indicated in the model, certain kinds of role perceptions lead to good job performance, while others lead to poor performance, although the data do not conclusively prove that a causal relationship exists.

The model predicted that role perceptions will lead to behavioral differences and it was suggested that they may combine multiplicatively with ability and effort in causing behavior. A rough test of this proposition was made by looking for an interaction effect between the relationships of effort, role perceptions, and performance. Unfortunately, a precise measure of ability was not utilized in this study; therefore, this aspect of the model could not be completely tested. The results in general, though, are congruent with the view that a multiplicative relationship exists. There is, for example, a stronger relationship between role perceptions and performance for high than for low effort managers. Certainly, the idea of a multiplicative relationship is a prime topic for future research—research that might add a significant measure of ability and look for a three-way interaction among effort, ability, and role perceptions.

In a very real sense, both Riesman and Whyte ventured out on a limb with their speculation about how business organizations function. Despite the fact that they had little empirical evidence to support their view that large-scale organizations, in particular, tend to reward the "other-directed," "organization man" types, it gained a broad, rather uncritical acceptance. Their supporting evidence for this point of view came largely from unsystematic observation and anecdotes. One cannot help admiring their inventiveness in creating the picture of American business and society that they did, but one can question the validity of their speculations. The present study does just this by testing one part of the speculation of these authors. There are also other speculations by Riesman and Whyte that have not been tested either by this study or by others. However, the data that have been gathered in the present study indicate that the views of Riesman and Whyte about the kind of behavior organizations demand of successful managers were basically incorrect.

Relationship to Previous Research

The results generally support the viewpoint that managers with more inner-directed role perceptions, and presumably behavior, are rated highly by both themselves and, more importantly for the believers in "organization man" philosophy, by their superiors. This evidence, when considered together with the findings of Fleishman and Peters (1962), Porter (1964), and Roadman (1964), provides an effective refutation of the "organization man" concept. The present study, and the Fleishman and Peters study, found that managers with nonconforming, inner-directed kinds of perceptions and values were rated highest by their superiors. Roadman found that individuals who display inner-directed kinds of behavior are promoted more readily, as would be expected from the present study, since inner-directed kinds of role perceptions are associated with higher superiors' ratings. All of these findings point to the conclusion that organizations not only tolerate but even *reward* inner-directed thinking and behavior.

Porter's (1964) results also agree with those of the present study. His finding that higher level managers have more inner-directed role perceptions is replicated in the results of the present study. The results suggest that one reason for Porter's finding is that those managers who are rated higher, and presumably, therefore, get promoted to higher level jobs, are the managers with inner-directed role perceptions. Thus, it is not surprising that the higher levels of management contain more people with inner-directed role perceptions. However, the finding that better performers tend to have more inner-directed role perceptions may not account for all of the differences in role perceptions that exist among management levels. One can also assume that higher level jobs objectively demand more inner-directed behavior. If promotion of inner-directed managers were the only factor operating, the expectation would be that the highest rated lower-level managers would have role perceptions that would approximate those of the average performer at the middle management level. As Tables 5–1 and 5–2 show, the highest rated performance group at the lower level is slightly less inner-directed than are the lowest rated managers at the middle level of management. Thus, it is probable that *both* the different kind of job and the selection of a certain kind of person bring about the finding that higher level managers have stronger inner-directed role perceptions.

The "Organization Man" Past and Present

In summary, it appears from the evidence that if there is a place for the other-directed, "organization man" type of manager in today's corporation, it is at a low level, one above which he is unlikely to rise. At this point one is tempted to wonder what led astute observers such as Riesman and Whyte to come up with theoretical points of view that are in disagreement with the current evidence, and why these views were and are so readily accepted by the general public. The most obvious reason is that there was an almost complete lack of any evidence at the time their books were written. Also, Riesman, in particular, was interested in building an entire view of our society. His views of industry were only a small part of his thinking. Furthermore, it may be, as is frequently suggested, that business no longer abounds with great individualists like Ford and Rockefeller. The statement is often made that Henry Ford couldn't get a job with the Ford Motor Company today, and it may well be true, although our evidence does not test this point. It probably is true that large-scale organizations are much less willing to tolerate the extreme deviant today than-they were 30 years ago. The observation of this trend probably contributed to Riesman's and Whyte's putting forth their viewpoints. However, the evidence indicates that to equate a tendency in organizations to be unwilling to tolerate an extreme deviant with accepting and rewarding only other-directed behavior and thinking would be wrong.

A factor that probably has led to the general acceptance of Riesman's and Whyte's views has been the tendency for the number of low level white-collar jobs to increase in many organizations. As indicated, these low level jobs probably do demand more other-directed kinds of behavior, but again it would appear fallacious to assume that the increase in these jobs indicates that organizations demand or reward strongly other-directed behavior elsewhere in the organization. Thus, although both Riesman and

Whyte may have been correct in noting an increasing trend in business to expand the number of lower level, other-directed, white-collar jobs and not to hire the extreme deviant, the implication that they appear to have drawn from these trends about the place of the inner-directed person in business has not been supported by the available objective evidence.

CHAPTER 6

Need Fulfillment and Need Satisfaction

Does job satisfaction improve job performance? The question is a venerable one in industrial psychology. Ever since 1932, when Kornhauser and Sharp made the pioneer study in this area, psychologists have been trying to determine whether increased morale or job satisfaction caused or contributed to improved job performance, or, indeed, whether the two sets of variables were related in any fashion to each other.

Through the 30's and 40's, most investigators implicitly assumed that good or high job satisfaction enhanced effective job performance and that the task for the researcher was to demonstrate this fact. Under the impact of the Western Electric studies and the rapidly emerging "human relations" movement, social scientists were prone to believe that if negative job attitudes could be eliminated or at least greatly reduced, a human brake on production could be changed into a positive force towards ever higher levels of output. Therefore, the search was motivated not only by scientific curiosity but also by some eminently practical considerations.

Interestingly, despite the repeated failures of most individual studies to come up with high, or even moderate, correlations between job satisfaction and job performance, no one thought to make a comprehensive review of the literature in this area until 1955. Furthermore, little or no attention was paid to the theoretical underpinnings of the relation between these two variables. The question of why one might expect high satisfaction to lead to high performance was never really examined in a rigorous, theoretical manner.

REVIEWS OF THE LITERATURE

As contemporary students of industrial psychology are well aware, naive thinking concerning this whole area was shattered in 1955 when Brayfield and Crockett published a long overdue systematic review of the empirical data. The key conclusion emerging from their article was that

. . . there is little evidence in the available literature that employee attitudes . . . bear any simple—or, for that matter, appreciable—relationship to performance on the job.

(They did go on, however, to point out that the data suggested a relationship in the expected direction between attitudes, on the one hand, and absences and turnover, on the other hand.) Another review of some of the same literature was completed by Herzberg and his associates at about the same time, although it was not made generally available until 1957 (Herzberg *et al.,* 1957). Herzberg and his colleagues took a somewhat more optimistic view of the empirical data than did Brayfield and Crockett. They stated:

. . . there is frequent evidence for the often suggested opinion that positive job attitudes are favorable to increased productivity. The relationship is not absolute, but there are enough data to justify attention to attitudes as a factor in improving the worker's output. However, the correlations obtained in many of the positive studies were low. (Herzberg *et al.,* 1957, p. 103).

(They also went on to point out, as did Brayfield and Crockett, that there was a definite trend for attitudes to be related to absenteeism and turnover.) As Katzell (1957) has noted, the chief reasons for the somewhat divergent conclusions reached by the two reviews was that they did not cover exactly the same literature, and that Brayfield and Crockett were less influenced by suggestive findings that did not reach statistical significance. In any event, the one conclusion that was obvious from both reviews was that there was not the strong, pervasive relationship between job satisfaction and productivity that many people felt to be the case before the available evidence was thoroughly examined.

Brayfield and Crockett not only reviewed the empirical evidence but went on to make a perceptive theoretical analysis. Their consideration of the theoretical issues involved led them to the following conclusions (among others) :

> Satisfaction with one's position in a network of relationships need not imply strong motivation to outstanding performance within that system, and . . . productivity may be only peripherally related to many of the goals toward which the industrial worker is striving. (1955, p. 421).

It is clear from the foregoing quotation that Brayfield and Crockett are essentially adopting a path-goal approach to the analysis of relationships between attitudes and performance. They see productivity as a means to goal attainment. If, in a given situation, productivity leads to the attainment of certain goals, a positive relationship between productivity and satisfaction might be expected. If, however, production does not lead to the attainment of important goals (i.e., goals that are seen as important by the employee) , then there is no reason to expect high productivity to be connected with high satisfaction. As the reader has gathered by now, this analysis by Brayfield and Crockett is in general agreement with the theoretical model presented at the beginning of this book.

About 10 years after the appearance of the Brayfield and Crockett article, Vroom carried out a new review of the literature in this area in his book, *Work and Motivation* (1964). Vroom confined his coverage to studies that presented results in terms of correlations (rather than also including studies that reported results in terms of mean differences between different criterion groups) . Of the 20 studies cited by him, 7 were published subsequent to the Brayfield and Crockett work. Thus, Vroom's review includes a number of studies in common with the 1955 review, but also updates the coverage through 1963. Vroom found that the median correlation between measures of job satisfaction and one or more criteria of performance was + .14 for 23 cases. (Several of the 20 studies used more than one criterion of performance and hence the number of correlations reviewed was 23 instead of 20.) The magnitude of the median relationship or association is obviously not large, as Vroom points out. However, the consistency of the direction of relationship in these 23 cases is quite impressive, since 20 of the correlations are positive! By a sign test, such consistency would occur by chance less than once in a hundred times (even using a conservative two-tailed test of significance). Thus, looked at in one way, the latest review of studies measuring the relationship between satisfaction and performance shows a very tenuous association between the two variables; looked at in another way, however, it leaves one with the impression that we are dealing with something other than a whimsical chance phenomenon.

As Brayfield and Crockett did, Vroom went on to make a detailed theoretical analysis of the determinants of job satisfaction and job performance. His conclusion was that

> . . . job satisfaction is closely affected by the amount of rewards that people derive from their jobs and . . . level of performance is closely affected by the basis of attainment of rewards. Individuals are satisfied with their jobs to the extent to which their jobs provide them with what they desire, and they perform effectively in them to the extent that effective performance leads to the attainment of what they desire. (p. 264).

Again, Vroom's position is very close to the path-goal approach emphasized by Brayfield and Crockett and the theoretical position taken in this book. All of these conceptualizations treat satisfaction as primarily a dependent rather than an independent variable.

It must be clear from the foregoing discussion of the various reviews of the empirical literature that there is basis for either optimism or pessimism that job satisfaction is in fact related to job performance. We prefer to take the former position. In fact, our fundamental premise throughout our research has been that job attitudes must *in some way* be related meaningfully to job performance. Note that at this point we are saying nothing about whether either variable has a causal relationship to the other— only that they are meaningfully related. Our task in constructing our theoretical model has been to specify under what conditions we should expect these two variables to be related, and to provide a psychologically sound basis for such expectations. Our empirical task has been to determine whether such relationships actually exist. Before going on to state specific hypotheses based on our model, however, it is necessary to reiterate a point made in Chapter 1: virtually none of the previous studies has dealt with the job attitudes and job behavior of employees above the level of first-line supervisors. The possible significance of this point was mentioned in Chapter 2, and it will be discussed further in this chapter after we present our hypotheses and findings.

In the remaining portions of this chapter we will first state the hypotheses derived from our model that pertain to the relationships of performance to perceptions of need fulfillment and need satisfaction; this section will be followed by a presentation of the empirical data that provide evidence relevant to these hypotheses, and by a discussion of such results. The present chapter will not include any data concerning satisfaction with pay, since attitudes toward pay constitute a major portion of our study and require extensive separate treatment. Results dealing wih pay satisfaction, and their relevant hypotheses, will be taken up in the following chapter.

HYPOTHESES

As we noted in Chapter 2, the diagram of our model on page 17 of Chapter 2 shows a wavy arrow going from the variable "performance" to the variable "rewards." The wavy line is meant to indicate that differential performance *can* lead to differential rewards. Whether, and to what extent, high performance does *in fact* lead to high rewards is, of course, an empirical question. Nevertheless, we assume that most formal organizations, especially business enterprises, have as one of their major personnel policies (implicit, if not always explicit) that good performance will in some way be rewarded by the organization. This is not to say, however, that good job performance is the only way to receive rewards. For example, simple longevity of employment and consequent loyalty to the company, expressed in the concept of job seniority, frequently leads to rewards. Here the rewards are not given for quality of performance, as long as it is above some minimum acceptable level, but rather for duration of performance. Also, as we stressed in Chapter 2, the model does not imply that the only type of rewards a person receives from his job performance are those that are provided by the organization. It is perfectly possible, and probably quite common, for the individual to provide himself with what we call intrinsic rewards, based on his own views of what he gained directly from the performance of a task, regardless of whether or not the organization later on provides extrinsic rewards. At any rate, all that the model is saying is that quality of performance is one of the factors that can influence rewards and that most organizations attempt to implement such a policy.

Let us further assume that managers ordinarily will have some reasonable basis for judging the degree to which the organization has been rewarding them and the degree to which their jobs provide intrinsic rewards. Also, let us assume that they can and will express such judgments in answer to certain attitude questions such as, "How much opportunity for independent thought and action is there now connected with my management position?" As will be explained later on in this chapter, we refer to such attitudes as expressions of the degree of need *fulfillment* that an individual perceives himself receiving from his particular job assignment.

With this introduction, we can now state our first hypothesis relevant to this part of our investigation:

Hypothesis 6–A. Where organizations give differential rewards based on differential performance, the higher an individual is rated on the quality of his job performance by his superior, the greater will be his expressed degree of need fulfillment.

The major issue in testing this hypothesis for the particular sample of respondents obtained for the present study revolves around the question of whether the specific organizations from which we drew our sample actually provide differential rewards for differential performance. This we cannot ascertain with any degree of certainty. However, there are bases for expecting that that kind of condition is present to some degree for our sample. One such basis is the fact that our respondents are managers rather than rank-and-file workers. It seems apparent that, in general, most organizations have considerably more freedom to reward their managers differentially than they do their hourly employees (unless the latter are on incentive pay plans). Frequently, non-management employees are unionized, and hence the firm is restricted in administering individualized rewards to members of this segment of the organization, compared to the management segment. More importantly, even in nonunionized organizations (such as a governmental unit), the nature of management jobs compared to nonmanagement jobs generally offers the possibility for greater variance in performance as well as greater flexibility by the organization in providing differential rewards (especially in terms of prestige, autonomy in decision making, opportunity for individual growth, and the like).

If the above analysis is correct, this would indicate that fulfillment is generally more likely to be related to performance for managers than for nonmanagement employees. Since we do not have data for the latter type of employees, we cannot test this kind of prediction in this study. Therefore, we must test Hypothesis 6-A (and our other hypotheses) on managers only. With respect to our particular sample of managers, our knowledge of the five organizations involved leads us to believe that they explicitly attempt to link rewards to the quality of managerial performance. This does not, of course, mean that they necessarily are successful in carrying out their intentions; it only means that we know of no information that indicates they advocate some other policy or that there are obvious environmental obstacles to implementing it. On these bases, and in accordance with Hypothesis 6-A, we would expect performance differences to be related to differences in perceived need fulfillment.

As mentioned earlier in this chapter and in Chapter 2, we also assume that good job performance can provide a person with intrinsic rewards, in terms of his own feelings, regardless of whether the performance is subsequently rewarded by the organization. This should be especially true in the growth-type need areas. Almost by definition these types of needs are directly fulfilled by intrinsic, self-mediated rewards. The organization can play an important role in such fulfillment by providing increased *opportunities,* but it cannot supply the fulfillment itself. "Virtue is its own reward," as it were. If we assume that these self-administered intrinsic rewards are based on the employee's perception that he has done a good job (which, in an individual case, might be quite at variance with the superior's estimate of the performance), then self-ratings of performance should be related to feelings of need fulfillment. This chain of reasoning leads directly to our next hypothesis and its very important corollary:

Hypothesis 6–B: The higher an individual rates the quality of his own performance, the greater will be his expressed degree of need fulfillment.

Again, as we did following Hypothesis 6–A, we might make a further prediction to the effect that: Hypothesis 6–B is more likely to be confirmed for managers than for nonmanagement employees. The reasoning here would involve the assumption that management jobs, in contrast to nonmanagement jobs, by their very nature are relatively more likely to contain a higher percentage of challenging tasks leading to feelings of self-esteem and growth when the individual believes he has performed them well. Although we feel the logic behind this argument is basically sound, we are again in the position of not being able to test this kind of prediction with our present data, which were collected only from managers.

There is, however, an important corollary to Hypothesis 6–B that can be tested with our data. Because feelings of receiving need fulfillment can result from both extrinsic rewards given by the organization and from self-administered rewards, and because self-administered rewards in the higher-order need areas are not dependent upon the superior's or the organization's evaluation of the quality of the performance, we can state the following corollary to the above hypothesis:

Corollary to Hypothesis 6–B: An individual's expression of the degree of need fulfillment he receives from his job should be more strongly related to his own rating of the quality of his job performance than to his superior's rating of the quality of his performance, especially for higher-order needs.

Returning now to the model and its diagram, we can proceed to consider how performance relates to rewards (i.e., to need fulfillment in terms of our questionnaire data) compared to how it relates to need satisfaction. It will be recalled that we have defined need satisfaction as the difference between need fulfillment that is received and that which is expected (i.e., in our questionnaire, the difference between "How much is there now?" and "How much should there be?"). Clearly, the model shows that rewards (i.e., actual fulfillment) should be more directly connected to performance than to satisfaction. Actual fulfillment (as perceived by the individual) is a component of satisfaction but is not the sole determinant of it. As indicated on the diagram, the degree to which a person is satisfied depends upon how much his expectations of equitable rewards exceed his fulfillment. To the extent that a manager thinks that his superior is evaluating his performance highly he may have a higher expected equitable reward level than a person who thinks his boss places a low evaluation on his performance. Therefore, *if* perceived equitable levels of rewards are raised as a result of high performance evaluations, then a high-rated performer's satisfaction might not be any greater than that of a low performer. If perceived equitable levels of rewards are not raised as a result of high performance evaluations, then the high-rated manager should also be more satisfied (as well as more fulfilled) than the low-rated manager. Note that the model does not specify whether perceived equitable reward levels will be higher for high-rated managers. This depends on many factors not taken up in the model. In any event, the reward expectations for high-rated managers should not be any lower than those of low-rated managers. In this case we have:

Hypothesis 6–C: Ratings of the quality of an individual's performance by his superior will be related as strongly or more strongly to his expressed degree of need fulfillment as compared to his degree of need satisfaction.

The above hypothesis deals only with superiors' ratings of managers' job performance. In line with our previous discussion we should state separately this same hypothesis for self-ratings of performance. Such a hypothesis would involve three ratings by the manager: his estimation of the quality of his job performance, his estimation of the need fulfillment he is receiving from his job, and his estimation of the need fulfillment (equitable rewards) he should receive from his job. Logically, these three separate ratings ought to be highly related to each other (and, in fact, Hypothesis 6–B specifically proposed this for the first two of these three ratings) : if a manager feels he has done a good job, he is likely (due in part to self-administered intrinsic rewards) to feel relatively highly fulfilled, *and*—though this is not specified in our model—he is likely to *expect* relatively high fulfillment. Since satisfaction, as we have operationally defined it, is the degree of difference between expected equitable rewards and received fulfillment, then a man who highly rates his own performance is not necessarily more likely to be satisfied than a man who gives a lower rating to his own performance. The former will have high fulfillment but also probably will have high expectations, whereas the latter will have lower fulfillment but also probably lower expectations. If this is the case we can state Hypothesis 6–D:

Hypothesis 6–D: An individual's own ratings of the quality of his job performance will be related more strongly to his expressed degree of need fulfillment than to his degree of need satisfaction.

Performance, in our model, is not the only variable that might be expected to have a relationship with rewards received and with the satisfaction from these rewards. If we direct our attention to those variables which immediately precede performance in the diagram of the model, we can see that effort might be expected under certain circumstances to have an influence on the final two dependent variables. To the extent that effort is transformed into accomplishment it should be related to fulfillment and satisfaction. However, as the diagram of the model shows, and as we have already discussed previously in Chapter 2, the relationship of effort to performance is mediated by abilities and traits, and by role perceptions. If a manager's traits and abilities are high with respect to the tasks assigned to him, and if he perceives his role requirements relatively correctly, then higher levels of effort will result in higher performance which should lead to greater rewards. However, if the former conditions do not hold, then effort may be increased with little resultant impact on performance and rewards. Thus, we can see that the model predicts that though effort may be related to rewards, its relationship should be weaker than the more direct relationship between performance and rewards (providing, of course, that rewards are not given directly for effort rather than for performance.) Stated in formal terms we have:

Hypothesis 6–E: An individual's performance rating will be more strongly related to his degree of need fulfillment than will his effort rating.

Before turning to a discussion of our methodology and findings with respect to the hypotheses stated in this chapter, we should mention one other feature of our results that we will report in some detail. The six graphs to be presented in this chapter will show a breakdown of the results by type of need (security needs, social needs, etc.). This will permit an examination of not only the overall trends across all needs taken together, but also any differences that may appear by type of need. Although the model does not specify the types of needs (in terms of their fulfillment and satisfaction) that should be related most strongly to performance ratings, we can make certain predictions about such results that are consistent with the model. First, let us assume that high performers will be more likely than low performers to provide themselves with intrinsic rewards, regardless of whether the organization provides proportionate extrinsic rewards. Second, as discussed previously in this chapter, we can assume that higher-order needs such as autonomy and self-actualization have a stronger intrinsic reward component than lower-order needs. If these two assumptions are true, we should expect to find that (the fulfillment and satisfaction of) higher-order needs are at least as strongly related to performance as are (the fulfillment and satisfaction of) lower-order needs. Furthermore, to the extent that the organizations in our sample fail to provide extrinsic rewards in relation to performance (something that tended to occur for pay at least), we should expect to find that higher-order needs are actually more closely related to performance than are the lower-order needs. To repeat, such predictions are not contained directly in the model. However, they flow logically from additional assumptions we have made here and elsewhere in elaborating on various facets of the model, and thus they are consistent with it.

ATTITUDE MEASURES OBTAINED

The part of our questionnaire that measured need fulfillment and need satisfaction was identical with a questionnaire that has been used previously in a number of studies involving over 5,000 managers (Porter, 1964; Haire, Ghiselli, and Porter, 1966; Eran, 1966; Miller, 1966; Porter and Mitchell, 1967). It consisted of 13 items of the following form:

The *opportunity for independent thought and action* in my management position:

a) How much is there now?
   (min)   1   2   3   4   5   6   7   (max)
b) *How much should there be?*
   (min)   1   2   3   4   5   6   7   (max)
c) How important is this to me?
   (min)   1   2   3   4   5   6   7   (max)

The complete listing of the 13 items is contained in Appendix II. The items, though presented in a random order in the questionnaire, had been preclassified into one of five types of needs:

Security
Social
Esteem
Autonomy
Self-Actualization

The rationale for the construction of the questionnaire has been presented in detail elsewhere (Porter, 1962). The key feature of the design of the 13 items was to try to tap types of needs (indicated above) that would be relevant to Maslow's (1954) theory concerning the relative prepotency of different needs.

As shown above, for each of the 13 items three questions were asked:

How much (of the characteristic) do you now have in your job?
How much (of the characteristic) should you have in your job?
How important is this (characteristic) to you?

The answers to the first of these three questions for each of the 13 items were taken as the measure of need fulfillment. The difference in answers between the sound (the perceived equitable amount) and first (reality) of these questions was taken as the operational measure of need satisfaction. That is, the greater the amount by which "should be" exceeded "is now" in our findings, the greater is the *dis*satisfaction.[1] The answers to the third question—how important?—were taken as a measure of the importance of the various types of needs, but the results based on this last question are not included in our findings presented in this book, except in Chapter 4 where we explicitly considered the importance of pay.

TESTS OF THE HYPOTHESES

Our first hypothesis in this chapter—Hypothesis 6–A—stated that the higher an individual is rated on the quality of his performance by his superior, the greater will be his need fulfillment. This hypothesis was predicated on the assumption that the organizations in our sample attempt to give differential rewards to their managers in accordance with their performance. If this assumption were incorrect, then of course our hypothesis would not be confirmed. Let us see what the data showed. Figure 6–1 presents the results for the comparison on need fulfillment of those managers (across all five organizations involved in this part of the study) rated by their superiors as high on quality of job performance versus those rated as low. As can be seen from the figure, high-rated managers reported more need fulfillment in each of the five need areas. Although the difference in the security need area was not significant, the differences in the other four need areas either approached significance (as in the case of social and esteem needs) or achieved significance (as in the autonomy and self-actualization need areas). It appears, then, that Hypothesis 6–A was generally confirmed, especially in the two highest-order need areas.

The results shown in Figure 6–1 represent still another area of our findings in which attitudes *are* significantly related to performance for this particular sample of managers. Whether we would have found the same attitudes-performance relationship for rank-and-file employees in the companies represented in our study is, of course, a matter for conjecture. However, if we couple our findings reported here with the relevant findings in previous studies that are summarized in various reviews of the literature,

---

[1]In the very small percentage of cases where "should be" responses were less than "is now" responses, the differences in that direction were arbitrarily treated as indicating even less dissatisfaction than zero differences.

we have some basis for believing that the relationship would have been weaker.

Whereas Hypothesis 6–A dealt with perceived need fulfillment in relation to superiors' ratings of the respondents' job perfor-

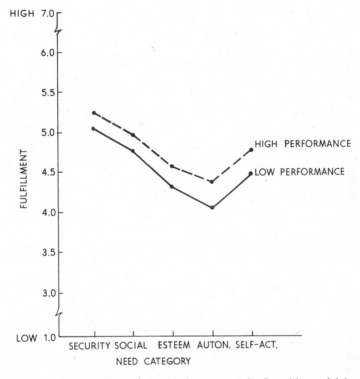

Figure 6–1. Need fulfillment in relation to superiors' rankings of job performance.

N: Low performance = 126; High performance = 134. Comparisons (by need category)—Security, Low (5.03) vs. High (5.23); n.s. Social, Low (4.79) vs. High (5.00): n.s. Esteem, Low (4.41) vs. High (4.58): n.s. Autonomy, Low (4.05) vs. High (4.39): $t = 2.43$, $p < .01$. Self-actualization, Low (4.47) vs. High (4.78): $t = 2.05$, $p < .05$.

mance, Hypothesis 6–B deals with fulfillment in relation to managers' self-ratings of their performance. This hypothesis predicts that individuals who rate the quality of their performance as relatively high will express greater need fulfillment than those who rate their performance as relatively low. The results pertinent to this hypothesis are shown in Figure 6–2. Here we can see that the "high" performance group reported significantly greater need fulfillment in all need areas except security (where there was little difference between the two groups). For the four need areas other than security, the differences were significant beyond the

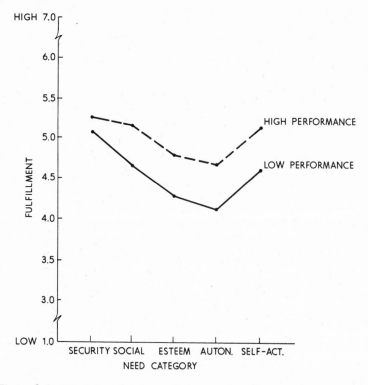

Figure 6-2. Need fulfillment in relation to self-ratings of job performance. N: Low performance $= 75$; High performance $= 70$. Comparisons (by need category)—Security, Low (5.09) vs. High (5.26): n.s. Social, Low (4.61) vs. High (5.15): $t = 3.87$, $p < .01$. Esteem, Low (4.26) vs. High (4.77): $t = 2.62$, $p < .01$. Autonomy, Low (4.10) vs. High (4.66): $t = 3.15$, $p < .01$. Self-actualization, Low (4.59) vs. High (5.11): $t = 2.68$, $p < .01$.

.01 level of confidence. Hypothesis 6–B, clearly, was confirmed by our data. Managers who feel that they are doing an especially good job also feel that their job is providing them with a high degree of need fulfillment. To what degree these feelings of fulfillment are due to actions of their immediate superiors and to the organization, and to what degree they are due to intrinsic feelings arising directly from the "doing" of the job, are questions that our data cannot answer. We simply know that if managers believe they are performing quite capably they also believe they are obtaining a high level of rewards, from whatever source.

As a follow-up to Hypothesis 6–B, we stated a corollary which proposed that managers' feelings of fulfillment would be related more strongly to their own evaluations of their performance than to their superiors' evaluations, especially for higher-order needs (e.g., autonomy and self-actualization). The logic behind this corollary was that if managers themselves feel they have done a good job, this provides a direct form of intrinsic rewards, at least in certain need areas, whereas superiors' views of the quality of subordinates' performance may not always be translated into actual rewards for those under them.

Thus, it was expected that fulfillment feelings would be tied more closely to managers' own ratings of how well they were doing than to the ratings made by their bosses. We have no direct statistical test of this corollary. However, by comparing the results from Figure 6–1, for superiors' ratings, to those from Figure 6–2, for self-ratings, it is possible to ascertain whether or not there is a trend in the anticipated direction. Such a comparison shows that for each set of ratings the "highs" differed from the "lows" in four of the five need areas. However, the t-values were definitely greater for the self than for the superiors' ratings, and the t-values tended to be largest for the higher-order needs. This indicates that the relationship between fulfillment and performance was somewhat stronger when managers rated themselves than when they were rated by their bosses. Thus, Corollary 6–B tends to be confirmed.

Our next hypothesis compared need fulfillment to need satisfaction in terms of their relative strength of relationship to superiors' ratings of performance. The model, and hence Hypothesis 6–C, predicts that the relationship of performance ratings to need fulfillment will be as strong as or stronger than the relationship of performance to satisfaction. To test this hypothesis requires that we consider a new graph, Figure 6–3, and compare it to the previously discussed graph, Figure 6–1. Figure 6–3 presents the findings for high- and low-rated managers (in terms of their bosses' estimations of their performance) in relation to their degree of *dis*satisfaction. This figure shows that low-rated managers were significantly more dissatisfied than high-rated managers in four of the five need areas. In other words, the lower a manager's performance is rated by his boss, the more likely the manager is to express dissatisfaction in a number of need areas. Now, let us compare the picture given in Figure 6–3 with that previously

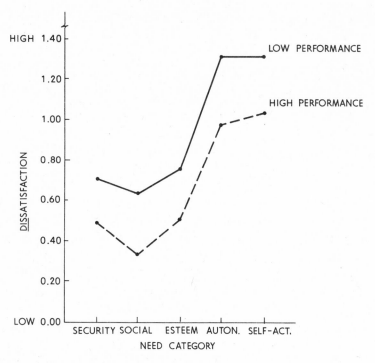

Figure 6–3. Need dissatisfaction in relation to superiors' rankings of job performance.

N: Low performance = 126; High performance = 134. Comparisons (by need category)—Security, Low (0.71) vs. High (0.49): n.s. Social, Low (0.62) vs. High (0.34): $t = 2.73$, $p < .01$. Esteem, Low (0.76) vs. High (0.51): $t = 1.81$, $p < .05$. Autonomy, Low (1.31) vs. High (0.97): $t = 2.80$, $p < .01$. Self-actualization, Low (1.31) vs. High (1.02): $t = 2.36$, $p < .01$.

shown in Figure 6–1. Before we do, however, let us also be sure to note that the scales along the ordinates are *not* the same in the two figures. The ordinate in Figure 6–3 is a scale of dissatisfaction (i.e., expected equitable fulfillment minus received fulfillment), while the ordinate in Figure 6–1 is a scale of fulfillment. Because of this, therefore, we cannot simply take the apparent (visual) separation between the "highs" and "lows" in the two graphs to test the adequacy of the hypothesis. We must, instead, compare the *t*-values for the differences between the two groups for each need in the two graphs. If we do this, we can see that Hypothesis 6–C tends to lack confirmation, mainly because the expectations of equitable rewards of the high performers were essentially the same as those of the low performers. High and low performers are slightly more separated (statistically speaking) on their dissatis-faction than on their fulfillment.[2] However, the differences in separation do not appear to be great. The safest conclusion is that performance differences among managers are about equally asso-ciated with satisfaction as they are with fulfillment.

Shifting from the relationship between satisfaction and the su-perior's rating of job performance to the relationship between satisfaction and the manager's self-rating of his job performance, we can examine Figure 6–4. This figure, along with Figure 6–2, is relevant to Hypothesis 6–D. This hypothesis predicted a stronger relationship between fulfillment and self-ratings than between satisfaction and self-ratings. A comparison of Figure 6–2 for ful-fillment and Figure 6–4 for satisfaction shows that the hypothesis was confirmed. In all five need areas except security needs, the relationships to fulfillment were significant, while those to satis-faction clearly were not significant. In other words, these results indicate that when a manager feels he has done a good job, he is likely to feel that he has been relatively highly rewarded (through a combination of extrinsic and intrinsic rewards), but he is no more likely than anyone else to be more satisfied with this level of rewards. The reason for this is that his perceived equitable level of rewards is also higher, and hence his degree of dissatisfaction with what he is receiving is just as great as for the man who is receiving less in the way of rewards.

Finally we come to Figures 6–5 and 6–6 which, combined with two previous figures (6–1 and 6–2), provide the data relevant to Hypothesis 6–E. It will be recalled that this hypothesis predicted that performance ratings would be more strongly related than effort ratings to managers' expressed degree of need fulfillment.

---

[2]The reason that the differences for dissatisfaction were statistically slightly greater than those for fulfillment was due to the slightly smaller variance in the dissatisfaction scores.

Such a hypothesis flows directly from the model, where it can be seen that more variables are assumed to intervene between effort and fulfillment than between performance and fulfillment. Hypothesis 6–E did not distinguish between self and superior's ratings of effort and performance. Thus, to test the hypothesis we

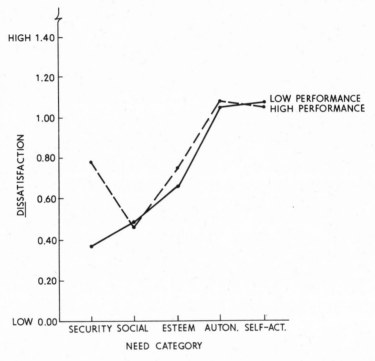

Figure 6–4. Need dissatisfaction in relation to self-ratings of job performance.

N: Low performance = 75; High performance = 70. Comparisons (by need category)—Security, Low (0.37) vs. High (0.79): $t = 2.03$, $p < .05$. Social, Low (0.48) vs. High (0.46): n.s. Esteem, Low (0.65) vs. High (0.74): n.s. Autonomy, Low (1.06) vs. High (1.09): n.s. Self-actualization, Low (1.07) vs. High (1.05): n.s.

can see if it is supported for each type of rating, or for one of the sets of ratings but not the other. First, let us examine the situation for supervisors' ratings. To do this, the reader is asked to compare the results shown in Figure 6–5 (for fulfillment in relation to effort) to those shown in Figure 6–1. Such a comparison shows that fulfillment was related significantly to each type of rating for certain of the need categories. Since there were more needs involved in significant or near-significant relationships for the performance ratings, there tends to be weak confirmation of the hypothesis for ratings made by superiors. If we make a similar comparison using self-ratings (i.e., comparing Figure 6–6 with Figure

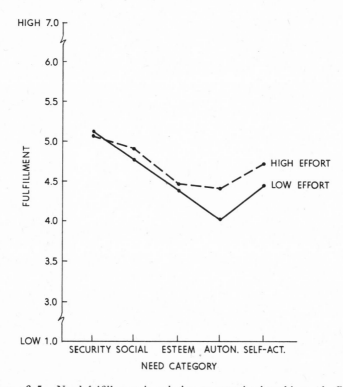

Figure 6–5. Need fulfillment in relation to superiors' rankings of effort.
N: Low effort $= 135$; High effort $= 136$. Comparisons (by need category)— Security, Low (5.11) vs. High (5.07): n.s. Social, Low (4.79) vs. High (4.91): n.s. Esteem, Low (4.40) vs. High (4.45): n.s. Autonomy, Low (4.02) vs. High (4.41): $t = 3.15$, $p < .01$. Self-actualization, Low (4.48) vs. High (4.72): $t = 1.66$, $p < .05$.

6–2) we see slightly the opposite trend. All five needs involved significant or near-significant relationships between self-ratings of effort and fulfillment, while only four of the five needs involved such relationships between self-ratings of performance and fulfillment. All in all, the total picture regarding Hypothesis 6–E is somewhat inconclusive. The hypothesis was not confirmed. Neither did the results go strongly in the opposite direction. At the moment, it appears that effort and performance show about equally strong (and positive) relationships to managers' feelings of need fulfillment, indicating that the organizations represented in our sample may be paying off on effort about as much as they are on performance.

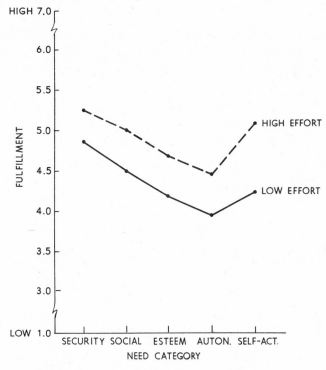

Figure 6–6. Need fulfillment in relation to self-ratings of effort.
N: Low effort = 83; High effort = 90. Comparisons (by need category)—Security, Low (4.88) vs. High (5.21): n.s. Social, Low (4.49) vs. High (5.00): $t = 2.58$, $p < .01$. Esteem, Low (4.18) vs. High (4.68): $t = 2.78$, $p < .01$. Autonomy, Low (3.93) vs. High (4.44): $t = 3.03$, $p < .01$. Self-actualization, Low (4.23) vs. High (5.08): $t = 4.62$, $p < .01$.

DISCUSSION AND IMPLICATIONS OF THE FINDINGS

The results presented in the preceding section indicate that the predictions based on the latter half of our model fared reasonably well, though not perfectly. We predicted significant relationships between certain types of attitudes and certain measures of performance, and in general we obtained such relationships.

More specifically, we began by predicting (Hypotheses 6–A and 6–B) that if the organizations in our sample were willing to provide rewards in relation to performance differences, then higher-rated managers should report greater need fulfillment than lower-rated managers. This was found to be true, both for superiors' ratings of performance and for self-ratings of performance. Further, we predicted (Corollary 6–B) that the relationships would be stronger for the self-ratings than for superiors' ratings. Again, this turned out to be correct. We next predicted (Hypothesis 6–C) that performance ratings by the superior would be related as strongly or more strongly to managers' reported need fulfillment as to their satisfaction with their fulfillment. The results with respect to this hypothesis were somewhat ambiguous, since superiors' performance ratings seemed to be slightly more closely related to managers' satisfaction than to their fulfillment. The differences in this direction, however, were minimal. The model was more successful in predicting (Hypothesis 6–D) that the relationship between managers' self-ratings of performance and their fulfillment would be stronger than the relationship between their self-ratings and their satisfaction. Finally, the model predicted that performance ratings would be more closely related than effort ratings to managers' feelings of need fulfillment. This failed to be confirmed, since effort and performance ratings seemed to be about equally strongly related to reports of need fulfillment.

In total, then, out of six testable predictions based on the five hypotheses and one corollary, four were confirmed and two were not confirmed. In no case, however, did the results turn out significantly in the opposite direction from that predicted. The picture we did obtain looks something like this (going from left to right in the diagram of our model) :

Though effort, in the model, is further removed from rewards (i.e., fulfillment) than is performance, we found this variable to be just as strongly related to fulfillment as was performance. We found, as predicted, that performance and rewards were significantly related. We also found performance and satisfaction related when the measures of performance are superiors' ratings, but not when the measures are self-ratings. Hence, the model's prediction that satisfaction is less closely related to performance than is fulfillment was upheld for self-ratings of performance but not for superiors' ratings.

Factors Affecting the Degree of Relationship between Performance and Satisfaction

The most important general aspect of our findings was that attitudes *were* related significantly to performance, as predicted by the model. We were able, therefore, to obtain results which have not always (or even often) been found in previous investigations dealing with this relationship. Why? To answer the question we can consider three factors which appear to be critical to such a relationship—the types of attitudes that were measured, the types of performance measures that were obtained, and the sample of employees. Let us examine each of these factors in turn.

Our attitude measures were somewhat different from typical job satisfaction questions in two major ways. First, instead of asking the respondent to indicate how well he liked some aspect of his work, or how satisfied he was with it, we asked him (in effect) to break this judgment into two parts: namely, how much (of some potentially desired reward) he was receiving, and how much (of this reward) he thought he should be receiving. The former answer we specified as "fulfillment" while the latter answer was used to help determine the degree of "satisfaction" by having the former answer subtracted from it. Forcing the respondent to make these two separate judgments, rather than the typical single judgment, enables us to see whether fulfillment might be more closely related to performance (as the model would predict) than would satisfaction. In fact, this turned out to be the case when we used self-ratings of performance, but there failed to be a distinction between fulfillment and satisfaction in their relationships to performance when the performance measure was the boss's ratings. Given these findings, therefore, our conceptual (and operational) separation of fulfillment as an attitude variable from satisfaction as an attitude variable does not seem to have accounted for our positive attitude-performance relationships.

The other respect in which our need satisfaction measures

differed from the usual job satisfaction questions lies in their content. Typically, most studies of job satisfaction have focused on either (a) a global question concerning satisfaction (e.g., "How satisfied are you with your job?—Very Satisfied, Moderately Satisfied, . . .") or (b) questions concerning characteristics of the environment (e.g., "How satisfied are you with your supervision?" "How satisfied are you with your working conditions?" etc.) . Our approach has been to focus on nonglobal questions. More specifically, we concentrated on a person's needs rather than on external aspects of the environment. This meant that we placed relatively more emphasis on intrinsic rewards (e.g., questions in the self-actualization area) than has typically been the case with previous research investigations in this area. In the terminology made popular by the research work of Herzberg (1959), we emphasized "motivators" as well as "dissatisfiers." As the reader has noted, the graphs of our findings presented the results by type of need so that one could compare the relationships between performance and more intrinsic-type rewards, such as self-actualization feelings, with the relationships involving more extrinsic-type rewards, such as security and social need satisfaction. As could be seen from these graphs, the results did vary somewhat by type of need. We shall reserve for a later part of this section an extensive discussion of the possible implications of these differences by type of need; at the moment, we merely wish to point to the existence of such differences as an indication that focusing on *needs*—especially higher-order needs—may have contributed to the fact that we obtained significant performance-attitudes relationships. As will be brought out later, this becomes an especially crucial point when we consider that our data were obtained from a managerial rather than a nonmanagerial sample.

Our performance measures were not particularly unique. Certainly, ratings by superiors are one of the most commonly used criteria of job performance in studies of this type. In our investigation, superiors' ratings, which were really rankings converted into standard scores, were simple and straightforward. However, we went beyond the collection of just superiors' ratings of performance and obtained three other sets of ratings that are not so frequently employed in this type of study: superiors' ratings of the "effort" put forth by their subordinates, self-ratings of performance, and self-ratings of effort. To be sure, superiors' ratings of effort were correlated with their ratings of performance, and self-ratings of effort were correlated with self-ratings of performance. Nevertheless, the correlations were far from perfect and hence the three additional sets of ratings allowed us to be somewhat more precise in the analysis of our findings than would otherwise have been the case. More importantly, they allowed us to make quite specific predictions based on our conceptual model. As it turned out, in the data reported in this chapter the theoretical distinction between effort and performance did not result in crucial differences in our findings. Both variables were about equally strongly related to appropriate attitude measures. The distinction between self-ratings and ratings made by others (i.e., superiors) had more of an impact. Self-ratings of performance were more closely related to rewards (i.e., fulfillment) than were superiors' ratings. The more important point, though, is that both sets of performance ratings were significantly related to the attitude measures. Therefore, if we had obtained only the usual single set of ratings, i.e., superiors' ratings of performance, we still would have obtained statistically significant attitude-performance relationships. This indicates that although the kinds of performance measures we used were valuable for analytic purposes, they were not the feature of our investigation that led to significant relationships of performance to fulfillment and satisfaction.

The third factor that may have contributed to these relationships involves the nature of our sample—especially the types of jobs held by respondents in the sample. Specifically, we are referring to the fact that we investigated the performance and attitudes of managers rather than rank-and-file employees. Let us examine how this factor might have influenced the nature of our findings.

If differences in performance are to be found related to differences in, say, perceived fulfillment, the environment must permit or allow variation to occur on both variables. To take up the performance side first, it seems reasonable to assume that management jobs are more likely to be constructed in such a way as to permit wider variations in performance than are nonmanagement jobs. For one thing, physical equipment is not as likely to place rigid ceilings on performance as would be the case in many rank-and-file jobs. Probably more important, however, is the fact that the duties and activities in management jobs are not as rigidly prescribed and defined when compared with typical nonmanagement jobs. If this is true, then the nature of managerial jobs would seem to provide more opportunity for unusually outstanding, innovative, and creative performance on the one hand, or distinctly poor performance on the other. (Over the long run, of course, managers who perform quite poorly will likely be weeded out of the organization; however, over the short run, and because of the less tangible nature of their duties, they are less likely to be dismissed as quickly as poorly performing nonmanagement employees who have obviously and visibly failed to meet some concrete and specific performance criterion.)

On the fulfillment or satisfaction side of the performance-fulfillment relationship for managers compared to nonmanagers, we need to look at the amount of variation possible in the reward systems of organizations. The reason for this is that fulfillment and satisfaction are presumed to reflect the amounts of rewards a person feels he is receiving in a given situation. To look at rewards, let us first consider the case of extrinsic rewards.

It is our contention that in an average industrial or business situation it is relatively easier for superiors to provide differential extrinsic rewards to managerial employees than to rank-and-file workers. For one thing, many nonmanagement employees work under contracts that provide for uniform wage rates for certain jobs. Thus, the only way an organization can reward someone with more money or more responsibility is to promote him into a higher-paying job. But how easily is this accomplished? In particular cases it obviously is accomplished, as, for example, when a man is promoted to a supervisor's job. In many such cases, however, the flexibility of the organization is limited. It is limited because there are relatively few supervisory openings or other types of openings among higher-level, nonsupervisory jobs. Thus, even though a superior may have no trouble in recognizing who his outstanding workers are, he frequently will have great difficulty in altering the reward structure to provide tangible evidence of his ratings. The situation should be entirely different, of course, where rank-and-file employees are on an incentive pay plan that is linked to variations in performance. In such cases as this, we might expect satisfaction (with pay) and performance to be positively related, since the organization is specifically trying to give rewards that are tied to performance.

In contrast to the jobs for rank-and-file workers, managerial jobs are not covered by contracts. If the organization wishes to pay varying salaries to several managers (in accord with the quality of their performance) who are all carrying out the same tasks, it is relatively easy to do so. Thus, rates of pay are much more flexible in management than in nonmanagement jobs. Furthermore, the managerial situation also provides greater flexibility in dispensing nonmonetary extrinsic rewards. For jobs at the same level in an organization there frequently is wide variation in the amount of status, responsibility, and autonomy provided. Therefore, even if an organization's budget prevents top management from providing as large monetary rewards as they might like for lower-level managers, they often are in a position to transfer a manager from one job to another in order to provide additional rewards of a nonfinancial variety. In sum, then, the generally greater number of alternatives available to the organization to reward managers extrinsically means that a greater potential exists for the manager to receive such rewards in relation to his level of performance than for the nonmanagement worker.

The situation for intrinsic rewards is much the same as for extrinsic rewards. Basically, there is greater opportunity for the manager—because of the nature of managerial jobs—to feel rewarded intrinsically in proportion to his efforts and performance than there is for the rank-and-file employee. Managerial jobs ordinarily involve much greater variety and opportunity to obtain a feeling of completion and of self-realization. Certain highly skilled nonmanagement jobs would be of this same type, but many such nonmanagement jobs would not. This being the case, it seems apparent that there is a high likelihood of many a rank-and-file employee working hard and performing well and, at the same time, feeling that he is not getting much in an intangible way from his job. The same thing clearly could happen in management. We are assuming, however, that the probability of this occurring, while not close to zero, is still much less in management.

For the past several pages we have been examining some of the possible reasons why we obtained significant performance-satisfaction relationships when such relationships have not been regularly obtained in the many studies addressed to this topic. We have attempted to indicate that certain factors—particularly the managerial nature of our sample of respondents—that were present in this investigation increased the likelihood that we would obtain positive associations between these two types of variables. At this point, it is important to turn the question around and ask: What factors in our study prevented us from obtaining much stronger performance-satisfaction relationships?[3]

Probably the chief reason why we did not obtain considerably stronger relationships between these variables involves the reward practices of the companies involved, as opposed to their reward policies. As we mentioned earlier in this chapter, the reasons why we felt Hypothesis 6–A (that performance would be related to perceived need fulfillment) would be confirmed for our sample were that these organizations endeavored to provide rewards in relation to merit and there were no obvious environmental obstacles to prevent them from doing it. Thus their reward *policies* were in accord with the direction of our prediction. However, the fact that the performance-satisfaction relationships were not higher than they were leads us to believe that these organizations, by and large, were not successfully implementing these policies. In effect, their reward *practices* were not strongly congruent with the policies. They were professing to link rewards to performance, but they apparently were allowing so many other factors to influence their compensation practices that performance-reward connections were attenuated. (Some evidence for this line of reasoning is presented in the next chapter in connection with the relationship of one type of extrinsic reward—pay—to performance ratings.)

We shall have considerably more to say on this point in our

---

[3] If our mean differences in satisfaction (and fulfillment) between high and low performance groups are converted into correlation coefficients, these coefficients are consistently larger than the median figure of .14 that Vroom (1964) reports in his review of correlational studies of performance-satisfaction relationships. However, the magnitudes of the associations that we obtained are not significantly higher in all cases, and they are not generally large in an absolute sense (i.e., above .40).

final chapter. For now, we can sum up our analysis by reiterating that it was probably the fact that we sampled managers rather than rank-and-file workers that resulted in significant performance-satisfaction relationships being obtained; it was probably the ineffective efforts of the organizations in tying rewards closely to performance that prevented the obtainment of substantially higher relationships. In any future studies of satisfaction-types of attitudes in relation to performance, we would predict that the two variables are more likely to be found positively related for managers than for nonmanagers, but the magnitude of such relationships for either sample will be strongly affected by the actual reward practices of particular organizations.

Variations in Performance–Satisfaction Relationships by Type of Need

Finally, in this section, we want to discuss briefly our results concerning the variations in performance-attitudes relationships by type of need. That is, do the relationships between, say, performance and fulfillment, seem to be stronger or in a different direction for one type of need than for another? A review of our graphs shows this: in those five graphs (all except Figure 6–4 for the relationship of managers' own ratings of performance to their dissatisfaction) where significant attitude differences might have been expected between high and low performance groups or between high and low effort groups, we get a picture that is depicted in the accompanying table. This table indicates that the

TABLE 6–1

Frequency of Occurrence of Levels of Significance of Differences between High and Low Performance Groups, or between High and Low Effort Groups, by Type of Need, for Figures 6–1, 6–2, 6–3, 6–5, and 6–6

Level of Significance	Security	Social	Esteem	Autonomy	Self-Actualization
.01	0	3	2	5	3
.05	0	0	1	0	2
.10	1	1	1	0	0
NS	4	1	1	0	0

two highest-order needs, autonomy and self-actualization, accounted for most of the highly significant $(p < .01)$ relationships and none of the nonsignificant relationships. That is, autonomy and self-actualization together produced eight relationships significant at the .01 level and none at the nonsignificant level, while the security, social, and esteem need categories taken together produced only five of the relationships significant at the .01 level and six of the nonsignificant relationships.[4] The summary table seems to indicate that performance differences were more likely to be related to attitudes concerned with such things as opportunity for personal growth and development, and opportunity for independent thought and action, than to attitudes concerned with the opportunity to form close friendships or the feeling of security one gets from his job.

Our model, as noted earlier, did not directly specify predictions by type of needs. However, assumptions consistent with the model allowed us to anticipate the kinds of findings we did obtain concerning differences among types of needs. Such findings could have both theoretical and practical implications. On the theoretical side they could mean that the *intrinsic* rewards potentially available in some job situations (e.g., many managerial jobs) have not been tapped sufficiently by questionnaires measuring job attitudes in previous investigations of attitude-performance relationships. Perhaps psychologists have been focusing too much on certain extrinsic rewards (pay excluded) such as status, friendly working companions, and physical job conditions in constructing their attitude measuring devices. In Herzberg's (1959) terms, they may have had relatively too many hygienic attitude items in their questionnaires which prevented the obtainment of significant attitude-performance relationships. On the practical side, if our results concerning differences among needs are substantiated by

---

[4] A certain caution should be noted here. Autonomy was measured by four items and self-actualization by three items, whereas security was measured by one item, social by two items, and esteem by three items. Hence, the latter categories would be measured with less reliability than the former two because of fewer items per category. However, although this statistical artifact undoubtedly did affect the results, it is not the entire explanation. Note the difference between esteem and self-actualization, both categories having three items each. Also note that the social category did as well as or better than the esteem category, even though it had only two items rather than three.

further research, this would have implications for the reward policies of firms. The nature of these possible implications will be spelled out in detail in our concluding chapter. It is enough, for now, to draw attention to the fact that our most statistically significant findings for need fulfillment and need satisfaction attitudes occurred in those need areas most directly reflecting the intrinsic rewards available in jobs. Such a result also lends further credence to the importance we attached to the nature of our sample as an explanation for obtaining generally significant attitude-performance relationships. Managerial jobs, to a much greater extent than nonmanagerial jobs, provide differential opportunities for receiving rewards in the autonomy and self-actualization need areas.

CHAPTER 7

Satisfaction with Pay

As mentioned in the introduction to the preceding chapter, we have purposely saved our data concerning the relationship of performance to pay satisfaction for separate treatment in the present chapter. The reason for this is that for this particular reward we have collected objective data on the actual amount received, as well as attitudinal data on the perceived amount received (i.e., the perceived "fulfillment"). Thus, in contrast to the preceding results concerning fulfillment and satisfaction of various lower- and higher-order needs, we can consider the relation of performance to each type of measure (i.e., actual and perceived) of "rewards" (variable #7), and each of these in turn to "perceived equitable rewards" (variable #8) and "satisfaction" (variable #9).

PREVIOUS RESEARCH

Before going further, however, let us briefly examine the nature of the findings of previous research in this area. Although there have not been a large number of investigations reporting results on the relationship of job performance to satisfaction with pay, the evidence, such as it is, indicates the existence of a low positive relationship. For example, two of the early Michigan leadership studies (Katz *et al.,* 1950; Katz *et al.,* 1951) found a low and nonsignificant positive association between satisfaction with pay and productivity. Also Herzberg, Mausner, and Snyderman (1959) claim to have found a relationship between dissatisfiers and their measures of productivity. According to their findings, dissatisfiers (e.g., when pay is unfairly low) frequently led to a reduction in quality of job performance. Although Herzberg *et al.* (1959) appear to feel the relationship is stronger than do Vroom (1964) and Brayfield and Crockett (1955), there is general agreement that satisfaction with pay and productivity are positively related.

Adams (1963; 1965) has stated a theory that makes predictions about the effects of perceived inequity of pay upon job performance. According to Adams, inequity exists when an individual's inputs (effort, skill, etc.) are not in balance with his outcomes—in this case, his pay. Dissonance (Festinger, 1957) arises because of this imbalance between the individual's expectations of what his pay should be and the reality of what his pay is. Adams' theory predicts that dissonance may cause an individual to reduce his inputs (e.g., lower his job performance), in order to bring them in line with his outcomes. The evidence that Adams has collected in support of his theory, however, is not directly relevant for the present study, since he has been largely concerned with the effects of perceived overpayment. Furthermore, although Adams' theory predicts that employees on a salary who perceive inequity in their pay due to underpayment should reduce their job performance, this part of his theory has not been adequately tested.

HYPOTHESIS

Let us return, now, to an examination of the part of our model that is relevant to the relationship between performance and satisfaction with pay. The chief difference between our model and the views of most previous investigators in this area (e.g., Herzberg *et al.*, 1959) lies in the hypothesized causal sequence. Typically, in the past, it has been common to think of satisfaction with pay as a factor causing or affecting performance. In contrast, our model suggests the reverse relationship as the more likely cause-effect sequence. Specifically, the model predicts that *if* (and this is a major "if" in most organizations, in our opinion) performance and actual pay are positively related to a high degree, then high performers should experience greater fulfillment. Additionally, if this high level of fulfillment is not accompanied by correspondingly high levels of expectation concerning what equitable fulfillment should be, then satisfaction should be relatively high and positively related to performance.

Before stating a formal hypothesis regarding these relationships, a more detailed analysis is necessary. First, it must be noted that our data provide two measures of performance (and effort), namely superiors' ratings and self-ratings. Since organizations presumably are more likely to give rewards in relation to the boss's estimation of a manager's performance instead of in relation to the manager's own self-ratings, we should expect to find that actual pay is more closely related to superiors' ratings of performance than to self-ratings. Next, one can look at the relationship between actual pay and perceived fulfillment with pay. Here, we should expect higher levels of actual pay to be related to higher fulfillment. The validity of this has been demonstrated in earlier research (Lawler and Porter, 1963) which showed that within any given level of management, higher pay was associated with perceptions of greater fulfillment and satisfaction. (It should be noted that in the Lawler and Porter study, measures of performance were not obtained, and therefore, it was not possible to determine whether performance and pay satisfaction were related.) High levels of perceived fulfillment, in turn, should lead to high levels of perceived satisfaction if expectations of equitable rewards (i.e., expectations of "how much should I receive?") are not correspondingly high. Since expectations concerning the amount of pay that ought to be received logically should be related more closely to self than to superiors' ratings of performance, we should anticipate pay satisfaction being more closely tied to superiors' ratings of performance than to self-ratings of performance.

All of the above considerations lead to the following formally stated hypothesis:

Hypothesis 7–A: Where organizations provide pay in relation to performance, and where an individual's perception of equitable pay is not influenced by the organization's performance evaluations, high levels of effort and performance will be related to high levels of satisfaction with pay.

TESTS OF THE HYPOTHESIS

To test this hypothesis, we can first examine the correlations between the job performance measures and the amount of actual pay received. These correlations are presented in Table 7–1, and they show relatively little relationship between actual salary and job performance, especially in the government sample. As expected, superiors' rankings are more highly correlated with amount of salary in the private sample than in the government sample; furthermore, as expected, the correlations in the private sample are higher for superiors' ratings than for self-ratings of performance. In the remainder of this section, only the results for the private sample will be discussed, because actual pay and performance measures were correlated almost zero in the government sample.

TABLE 7–1

Pearson Correlation Coefficients between Actual Pay, and
Superiors' Rankings and Self-Ratings on Job Performance
Measures[a]

	Actual Pay	
	Government Sample (N=237)	Private Industry Sample (N=236)
Superiors' Rankings		
Effort	.01	.20**
Quality of Job Performance	.00	.14*
Self-Ratings		
Effort	.06	−.11*
Quality of Job Performance	.04	.04

[a]Correlations computed separately for each management level and then averaged.
*$p < .05$
**$p < .01$

Since actual pay and the performance measures in the private sample were only weakly related (even though the relationships did reach statistical significance), we should expect, according to the hypothesis, to find that feelings of fulfillment will *not* be closely related to performance measures. The results bear this out. Figures 7–1 and 7–2 (for superiors' ratings and self-ratings of performance, respectively) illustrate that managers' feelings of fulfillment (i.e., answers to the question of "how much is there

now?") were only slightly higher for those rated high on performance compared to those rated low. Interestingly, managers' expectations about the amount of pay they should be receiving also
were not related to superiors' ratings of performance (Figure
7–1), but were related fairly strongly to self-ratings of perfor-

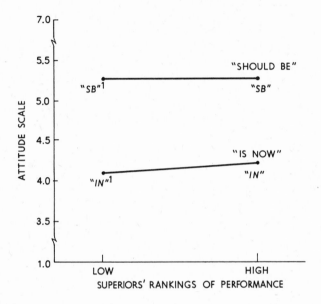

Figure 7–1. Need fulfillment ("Is Now") and perceived equitable reward
("Should Be") attitudes for high and low performing managers, as ranked
by superiors.
  N: SB[1] and IN[1] = 91; SB and IN = 104. Comparisons—SB[1](5.3) vs. SB(5.3):
n.s. IN[1](4.1) vs. IN(4.2): n.s.

mance (Figure 7–2). This latter finding indicates that managers'
feelings of equity with respect to their pay have relatively little
to do with their bosses' evaluation of them, but, as might be expected, are associated with their own self-evaluations.

  If dissatisfaction is taken to be the difference between perceived fulfillment and expected equitable fulfillment, then
Figures 7–1 and 7–2 show the following concerning dissatisfaction:
when the performance variable consists of superiors' ratings, dissatisfaction with pay is completely unrelated to performance.
When self-ratings constitute the measure of performance, the *high*
performance managers show somewhat *more dissatisfaction* than

the low performance managers. This latter finding occurs both because high performance was not related either to actual pay or to perceived pay, and because expectations concerning the amount of pay that should be received tended to be higher for the self-rated high performance managers.

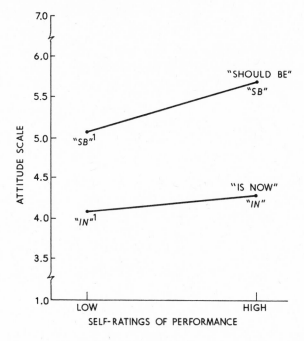

Figure 7–2. Need fulfillment ("Is Now") and perceived equitable reward ("Should Be") attitudes for high and low performing managers, as rated by self. N: SB[1] and IN[1] = 62; SB and IN = 55. Comparisons—SB[1](5.1) vs. SB(5.7): $t = 3.18$, $p < .01$. IN[1](4.1) vs. IN(4.3): n.s.

Hypothesis 7–A can now be evaluated in the light of the findings so far reported. Since high levels of performance were not related either to actual pay or perceived fulfillment, the hypothesis would predict no relationship between pay satisfaction and the performance measures. This is the finding that we obtained. We cannot, however, say that the hypothesis was confirmed, since it is not possible to prove statistically a hypothesis of no difference. Therefore, we introduced a new analysis to try to test Hypothesis 7–A. The hypothesis predicts definite differences in managers' satisfaction if their actual pay *is* related to their performance and if expectations about equity do not increase (proportionately) in relation to performance. To test this prediction, we took the private sample and eliminated all individuals for whom the amount of their actual pay was not related positively to their superiors' evaluations of their performance.[1] (Superiors' evaluations were used instead of self-evaluations because, as pointed out previously, there were no increases of expectations with higher ratings, whereas there were such increases with higher self-ratings). In other words, we now have a specific sample where actual pay is tied to performance, a necessary condition for the testing of Hypothesis 7–A. The results of the analyses on this sample are shown in Figure 7–3. This figure shows that managers rated higher in performance by their superiors perceive

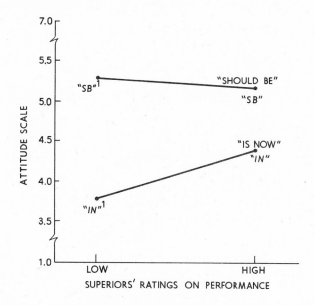

Figure 7–3. Need fulfillment ("Is Now") and perceived equitable reward ("Should Be") attitudes for those high and low performing managers (as ranked by superiors) whose actual pay is related to their performance.

N: SB[1] and IN[1] = 50; SB and IN = 62. Comparisons—SB[1](5.3) vs. SB(5.2): n.s. IN[1](3.8) vs. IN(4.4): $t = 3.13$, $p < .01$.

---

[1]This was accomplished by first dividing the sample into high and low pay groups. Then each of the two pay groups was divided into high and low performance groups, providing a total of four subgroups. For the subsequent data analysis, the "high pay–low performance" and the "low pay–high performance" subgroups were eliminated.

significantly $(p < .01)$ greater pay fulfillment, but do not expect greater pay, than managers rated lower in performance. It is clear from this figure, therefore, that high performance managers *are* significantly more satisfied with their pay than low performance managers. Thus, for this subgroup of managers for whom actual pay is tied to performance, Hypothesis 7–A is confirmed.

IMPLICATIONS OF THE FINDINGS

The most important practical implication of our findings concerning satisfaction with pay seems to be that if organizations hope to have ther pay incentive programs lead to a situation where their best managers are satisfied with their pay, they must first make sure that differences in pay are tied to differences in performance. Furthermore, they must make sure that individual managers *realize* that performance differences are the chief factor in determining whether their pay is relatively high or relatively low. This means, of course, that, relatively speaking, some managers will always be dissatisfied with pay. However, if organizations are successful in basing pay on performance, then this dissatisfaction will be concentrated among the relatively poor performers. For most organizations, this is not an undesirable state of affairs.

One other final note on our findings: superiors' ratings of effort seemed as closely related to actual pay as did superiors' ratings of performance. This suggests that for companies in our sample, pay is being dispensed at least as much for trying hard (i.e., effort) as for accomplishment (i.e., performance). The implication seems to be that some companies, in evaluating managerial performance, are failing to distinguish between managers' attempts at performance and their actual accomplished performance. We would always expect, as noted repeatedly in this book, that effort and performance would be positively associated. Nevertheless, we are somewhat surprised to find, in contrast to what our model would indicate, that these variables are more or less equivalently related to managerial satisfaction.

CHAPTER 8

Reevaluation of the Model, and Future Research Needs

The previous four chapters have reported the findings of our empirical investigations in considerable detail. Hence, in this chapter we shall not attempt an extensive review of these results. Instead, we will focus on a reassessment of the theoretical model in the light of the data we obtained relevant to the model; and, second, a discussion of future research needs pertinent to further development of the model.

A REASSESSMENT OF THE MODEL

In this section our concern will be with a broad overview of the conceptual model in relation to the findings obtained from our field research. Here we will not restate specific hypotheses derived from the model. Rather, we will look at the general pattern of relationships suggested by the model to determine whether it is supported by the empirical evidence. From our point of view, it is the *pattern* of results, rather than any single result, that is most important in examining the model.

Taken as a whole, our findings generally confirm the pattern of relationships implied by the model. Those variables presumed to affect performance turned out to show relations to performance, and those variables presumed to result from performance also typically were related to performance. To this extent, therefore, our findings validate the model. However, a crucial aspect of the model remains to be validated in future research. This aspect concerns the direction of *causality*. The model not only predicts certain patterns of relationships among the variables, but it also predicts the direction of cause-effect relationships. For this feature of the model, our data are only indirectly relevant because our findings are of an associative nature. Nevertheless, as will be discussed later, certain parts of our findings hold implications that can be used in inferring causality. For the moment, it is sufficient to state that the model has passed its first rough screening and at least holds promise for predicting cause-effect relationships.

A Summarized Review of the Findings

Let us first review our findings step-by-step in relation to the model. The first part of the model (refer back to Exhibit A on page 17) concerns the relationships among three variables: value of reward, perceived effort–reward probability, and effort. The data collected in our investigations that were most relevant to testing the relationships among these three variables were the data concerned with pay (Chapter 4). Data on the *value of reward* variable were obtained from questionnaire information on the importance of pay to the manager. To collect data related to the *perceived effort–reward probability,* questionnaire information was obtained on how closely the manager felt his pay was based on job performance factors (including effort). To collect data on *effort,* and also on *performance,* self-ratings and ratings by superiors were obtained. The model predicts that *value of reward* and *perceived effort–reward probability* combine to influence *effort* (and, in combination with *ability* and *role perceptions,* to influence *performance*). That is, where the value of a potential reward is high, and where the perceived probability that effort leads to this reward is also high, then effort should be high. Essentially, this is the nature of the findings involving pay. Managers who saw pay closely tied to performance factors received higher performance and effort ratings than managers who did not see such a close relationship (i.e., who had lower effort-reward probabilities). And, as the model clearly predicts, such reward probability types of attitudes related more closely to effort than to performance. Furthermore, the strongest relationships between perceptions of pay being based on performance factors and our measures of effort existed for those managers who attached the greatest importance to pay as a reward. This latter finding not only supports the model's contention that both *value of reward* and *perceived effort–reward probability* are involved in determining a manager's *effort,* but it also indicates that the form of the combination of these first two variables in the model is interactive rather than additive.

The next major set of relationships implied by the theoretical model involves the variables of *effort, ability, role perceptions,* and *performance.* The results most relevant to the interaction of these four variables were presented in Chapter 5. As previously indicated, measures of both *effort* and *performance* involved ratings by superiors and by the managers themselves. Data on *role perceptions* were collected by means of questionnaire items dealing with inner- and other-directed behavior requirements, but little information was obtained regarding *ability* in our investigations. The model indicates that each of these three variables (effort, abilities, and role perceptions) should have an impact on performance and that in combination they determine performance.

The basic results in Chapter 5 were focused on *role perceptions* and showed that particular types of such perceptions were significantly related to managerial performance. Even more importantly, in line with the model, the results showed that such role perception–performance relationships were stronger for managers who were seen as exerting high effort (i.e., were "highly motivated") compared to those seen as exerting relatively low effort. Thus, not only is the notion of a combined effect of *effort* and *role perceptions* on *performance* supported, but also the results indicate the relationship may well be an interactive one. In other words, if extremely high effort were to be combined with extremely inaccurate role perceptions, the prediction would be that the subsequent performance would be evaluated as relatively ineffective.

The final set of relationships dealt with by the model concern *performance, rewards* (fulfillment) , *perceived equitable rewards,* and *satisfaction.* Chapter 6 described our measures of the latter three variables in considerable detail. Rewards, other than pay, were measured by obtaining questionnaire information from managers concerning "how much" fulfillment they were obtaining with respect to various types of needs. The model predicts that *if* actual extrinsic rewards are given more or less in proportion to actual differences in performance, then perceptions of fulfillment should be related to performance differences. Perceptions of fulfillment, according to the model, do not, however, lead directly to satisfaction. The relation between *fulfillment* and *satisfaction* is modified by the individual's level of *perceived equitable rewards,* in that satisfaction is conceived as the difference between perceived equitable and actual rewards.

The findings reported in Chapter 6 showed that for our sample of managers and organizations, performance and feelings of fulfillment were related, *especially for higher-level needs,* whereas performance and satisfaction were significantly related only when superiors' ratings (and not self-ratings) constituted the measure of performance. However, the model's prediction that measures of performance would be more closely related to fulfillment than would measures of effort failed to be confirmed; fulfillment was about equally related to the two measures.

The findings on pay fulfillment and pay satisfaction were analyzed separately (in Chapter 7) from the other reward (need fulfillment) findings, since for this measure we not only had perceptions of fulfillment, but also objective data on the amount of salary received. For the total sample of managers, performance and satisfaction with pay were not related; however, such a finding was not contrary to the model since the relationship between performance and *actual* pay was insignificant for the government sample and relatively low (though significant) for the private sample. Beyond this fact, however, was the finding that performance and satisfaction with pay were quite significantly related when only those managers for whom performance and actual pay were related constituted the sample for analysis. That is, when performance differences were rewarded accordingly, performance and satisfaction with pay were highly related.

Revision of the Model

As we have indicated, the results on the whole tend to support the pattern of relationships as hypothesized by the model. At this point, given the results of our empirical study, there are probably two changes we would introduce into the model. The first change would involve the designation of the *reward* variable. We are now convinced that this variable should really be considered as two variables: *extrinsic rewards* (administered by the organization), and *intrinsic rewards* (administered by the individual himself). The results presented in Chapter 6—especially those concerning differences among types of needs—on fulfillment and satisfaction lead us to believe that this distinction between extrinsic and intrinsic rewards is more important than we had realized before we undertook our research. It now appears that those types of needs which can be satisfied primarily by intrinsic rewards—i.e., the higher-order needs such as autonomy and self-actualization—are more likely to produce attitudes about satisfaction that are significantly related to performance than are needs—such as security and social needs—which can be satisfied primarily by extrinsic rewards. A stronger relationship for the higher-order needs is predicted because of the closer relationship between rewards and performance where higher-order needs are involved.

In short, if we were now redrawing this part of the diagram of our model, we would divide variable #7—*reward*—into two variables: 7A, *intrinsic reward;* and 7B, *extrinsic reward.* These two types of rewards, rather than a single reward variable, would be conceived of as intervening between *performance* and *satisfaction.* For extrinsic rewards, there would continue to be a wavy line between performance and rewards, indicating that such rewards often are not, in fact, tied to performance. For intrinsic rewards, there would be a semi-wavy line. This is to indicate that a direct connection exists between performance and these rewards *if* the design of the job provides sufficient variety and challenge so that when a person feels he has performed well he can reward himself. If the design of the job does not involve these characteristics, then there would be no direct connection between good performance and intrinsic rewards. Thus, the degree of connection between performance and intrinsic rewards is dependent on the make-up of the job duties.

The second change would involve a link from *performance* to *perceived equitable rewards* to depict the fact that self-ratings of performance seem to act rather directly upon this variable. The data from our study clearly point out that higher levels of self-rated performance are associated with higher levels of expected equitable rewards. Our view, now, is that this comes about because the self-ratings of performance are a major influence on an individual's feelings about what levels of rewards he should receive as the result of his performance. In terms of our model, this relationship might be represented by a dashed line running from (the self-rated part of) *performance* to *perceived equitable rewards.*

The incorporation of the two changes discussed above would lead to a redrawn diagram of the model, which we show in Exhibit B. This exhibit represents our current state of thinking concerning the relationships among the variables considered in the model.

Causal Inferences

Before continuing, we should also mention two aspects of the model that cannot be directly evaluated with our own data. The first of these involves the question of causality. Although, as we have noted already, the causality implications of our model have not been tested by our data, nevertheless certain parts of our findings can be used tentatively to infer causality. For example, each of the following results lends inferential, but indirect, support for the causal sequences outlined in the model:

(From Chapter 4) : Attitudes concerning the determinants of pay are more closely related to ratings of effort than to ratings of performance.

(From Chapter 4) : The relationship between attitudes concerning the determinants of pay and ratings of performance is moderated by the importance attached to pay by the manager.

(From Chapter 5) : The positive relationship between inner-directed role perceptions and performance is greater for managers rated high in effort than for managers rated low in effort.

EXHIBIT B

Revised Diagram of the Theoretical Model

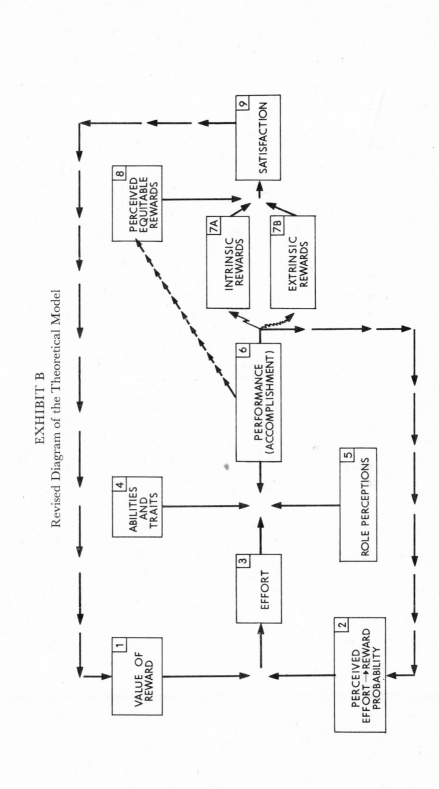

(From Chapter 7):   The relationship between performance and satisfaction with pay holds only for those managers for whom performance is directly related to their actual pay.

Each of the above findings, in itself, could be explained by some cause-effect hypothesis other than the one proposed by the model. However, taken together, the particular relationships summarized above would seem difficult to explain by hypothesizing cause-effect relationships of the opposite direction from those we propose— e.g., by hypothesizing that performance causes certain role perceptions or that satisfaction causes performance. In spite of this array of inferential evidence, however, we are still a long way from having conclusive evidence with respect to the cause-effect sequences in the model.

Feedback Loops

The other aspect of the model that could not be evaluated with our own data concerns the hypothesized "feedback" loops in the model. We did not collect the type of data that would enable one to determine in what way changes in levels of need satisfactions affect the future values of certain rewards, nor how increases or decreases in the strength of the performance-reward relationships affect managers' estimates of the probabilities of effort leading to rewards. Hence, this aspect of the model remains largely speculative at the moment.

FUTURE RESEARCH NEEDS

From the preceding discussion it is obvious that two basic kinds of data are needed in order to test the model further. First, data are needed that can determine the direction of causality in the relationships found to exist; secondly, data relevant to the feedback loops in the model are needed. In the following review of future research needs, we will begin by considering the issues involved in collecting these kinds of data, and then we will proceed to look at the possibilities for using improved measures of variables and broadened samples of subjects in future studies.

Need for Data to Test Causal Predictions

Evidence from our investigations concerning the causal nature of the relationships depicted in the theoretical model is almost totally inferential. The most important single research need for the future, in connection with the model, is to collect data that will provide evidence on the direction of causality. While this aim is easy to state, the generation of such evidence is more difficult. Situations in which field studies are carried out present tremendous obstacles to the researcher who endeavors to obtain such evidence, because of the difficulties involved in controlling extraneous variables. (For a good discussion of the problems encountered in conducting such field experiments, see Seashore, 1964). While highly controlled field experiments are almost impossible, approximations can be attempted by the deliberate introduction of certain changes in organizations, or by the before-and-after observation of natural changes taking place in them. For example, instances where firms are making definite changes in their managerial compensation policies—with respect either to pay or nonmonetary compensations—would provide ideal circumstances for the collection of data relevant to cause-effect relationships predicted by the model. Likewise, changes in the stated criteria by which managerial performance will be evaluated (e.g., a decreased emphasis on seniority accompanied by an increased emphasis on "merit") would provide other types of opportunities to study causal sequences.

Two other alternatives to attempted field experiments are available for producing data relevant to determining causality. One of these involves longitudinal studies. The chief difficulties with this type of study, of course, involve the relatively lengthy waiting period before results become available and the necessity of correctly selecting in advance the critical variables to be measured. This is where the existence of a conceptual model, such as the one presented here, is helpful. It provides the researcher with some definite leads about the kinds of variables on which he should collect data and also about the kinds of measuring instruments that would be appropriate. Specifically in connection with the model presented in this book, a longitudinal study that obtained repeated measures of attitudes concerned with reward values and effort-reward probabilities, and repeated measures of effort and job performance, could provide useful data for increasing our understanding of the probable cause-effect sequences.

Both longitudinal and field experimental studies could provide information on the hypothesized feedback loops in the model. Data from either type of study could help answer such questions as, how (or if) changes in actual performance-reward relationships affect an employee's perception of effort-reward probabilities. If continuous monitoring of satisfactions were included in a longitudinal study, it would be possible to see if changes in satisfaction levels precede changes in the degree to which a manager evaluates the desirability of different rewards. In any event, the need is great for information relevant to the hypothesized feedback loops.

The third major way to obtain data on cause-effect sequences implied by the model would be to conduct laboratory experiments. The chief difficulty here is in generalizing the results of such studies to the field situation. (For a thorough discussion of the problems and possibilities in generalizing from results from small group laboratory studies to statements applicable to real-life large formal organizations, see Weick, 1965.) Recent laboratory studies by Adams (1963, 1965) on the effects of pay inequities provide examples of studies that might be adapted to investigating particular cause-effect relationships derived from the model. Other examples could be experiments devised to alter, in a systematic way, performance-reward relationships, if such experimental manipulations were accompanied by measures of satisfaction, value of rewards, and perceived effort-reward probabilities.

Before taking up problems associated with measuring the different variables in our model, one other substantive need in future research studies should be noted. A major component of the model involves effort-reward probabilities. We investigated this type of probability only with respect to the reward of pay. This, clearly, is a limited approach to the effort-reward probability variable. Future research should be aimed at broadening the measurements to include other rewards, such as status, friendship, self-fulfillment, and so forth. Measures of negative outcomes and the degree to which they are seen to be related to effort and performance might also be included. If, as seems likely, negative outcomes are shown to have an important influence on performance, then the model should be extended to include more explicitly such negative outcomes and the perceived probability that they depend upon effort. These steps ought to allow for better prediction of job behavior from outcome-probability attitudes because more of the relevant influences on performance would be considered.

In one sense, managers' estimations of the probability of effort leading to such rewards might contribute something to the solution of the causality question—they would provide data on managers' *perceptions* of the causal relationships, whether or not these perceptions are "factually" true. While such data will not provide any ultimate solutions to the mysteries of causality, they will at least give us some better clues than we have now about where to look for causality.

Need for Improved Measures of the Key Variables

Our measures of certain of the variables in the model were relatively crude and, therefore, require improvement. For example, the measure of *value of reward* in our investigations consisted of obtaining simple ratings of the "importance" of various rewards to the individual. More sophisticated measures of reward value would undoubtedly permit more precise tests involving this variable. As to *effort-reward probability,* we have already mentioned that it may be desirable to include separate measures of the perceived effort-performance probability and of the perceived performance-reward probability. Almost completely absent in our study were measures of *ability*. With the wide variety of ability tests currently available, future research could relatively easily include sound measures of at least some of the abilities presumed to be involved in the practice of management. Our measures of *role perceptions* were limited to an exclusive focus on the inner-other-directed behavior distinction. Clearly, future investigations could and should include measures of other dimensions of this variable.

Some of the other variables in the model, such as performance, effort, and satisfaction, were measured with more completeness in our study. Even for these variables, however, improved measuring instruments can be developed. Managerial *performance*, for example, is not an easily measured variable and there are a variety of possible approaches that have been developed by researchers to attempt to study this variable. Perhaps no single measure of this kind of variable can be considered "best"; nevertheless, efforts at construct validation of this variable can be developed and eventually incorporated into tests of the model.

Effort is a variable that has received relatively little attention in the past from researchers studying the relationship of attitudes to performance, but it is a variable that has a crucial role in our model. It is our view that if researchers are ever to find meaningful relationships between attitudes representing measures of motivation on the one hand, and behavior on the other hand, they must look not only at measures of productivity or performance, but also at measures of effort. In other words, the focus should be on developing measures of attempted performance as well as the typical measures of completed performance (e.g., actual output) or accomplishment.[1] Although, as we noted in Chapter 3, measures of these two variables normally will be positively correlated, they are sufficiently different to require separate treatment.

Measures of *satisfaction* must include both the "equitable" component as well as the "actually received" component. Attitude instruments that simply ask the "how satisfied are you with . . .?" type of question obscure the operation of these two components. When an individual reports he is "satisfied," it is difficult, with

---

[1]An illustration of an attempt to get raters to focus on "effort" rather than "overall performance" in evaluating subordinates' behavior, is provided below by a set of rating scale instructions developed by a colleague of the authors, Vance Mitchell. His instructions (slightly rephrased) to raters were the following:

"The purpose of this section is to help us obtain a picture of how much of the effort and energy at their disposal managers feel they actually use in doing their managerial jobs. The full meaning of the self-evaluation we want from you is difficult to explain in a sentence or two. Perhaps the following will help in making it clear.

"Each of us has a limited amount of effort and energy at his disposal. We must share these resources among a number of different activities in our lives. Some of these activities call for more of our resources than others do. Our home and family, church, job, social organizations to which we belong, and other interests all claim their share. We meet these different claims as we think best, taking into consideration the need to earn a living, our own interests and preferences, our concern with and enthusiasm toward different

that type of question, to determine whether this is because he expected little and feels he is receiving little, or because he expected much and is receiving much. The psychological determinants and consequences in the two cases are probably different and, therefore, require the two-part determination of satisfaction. This we have attempted to do in our investigations, but other methods aimed at obtaining this type of satisfaction data can be developed which will improve upon our particular approach.

Turning to sampling considerations, we attempted to obtain a reasonably diverse group of managers by securing respondents from both business and government. Furthermore, in each of these two major subsections of our total sample we collected data from more than one organization. (Our industrial sample came from four companies, our government sample from three different units of state governments in two states.) Thus, our sample provides somewhat greater opportunities for generalization of findings than is the case in typical studies of management which often involve only a single organization. However, future research could be facilitated by a sharper focus on the types of organizations represented in a research sample. Specifically, a major aim of future research dealing with the general question of the relationship of attitudes and performance among managers should be to collect data from managers working in organizations with explicitly different reward policies. Perceptions of effort-reward probabilities and the actual performance-reward connections are

---

activities, obligations we may feel toward others, and a number of other factors. The result is far more than a simple schedule of our waking hours . . . it reflects how hard we really try at different things. One way of describing this is, *how much of ourselves* we really put into the time we spend in connection with various activities.

"For a number of reasons, the share of themselves different people put into doing their jobs may vary considerably. Some very effective managers 'put out' a great deal in connection with their jobs . . . the job seems to be the most important thing in their lives. However, we can also think of other highly effective managers who impress us as putting out only some fraction of the total effort which others appear to expend. *Please note,* we are *not* talking about *how well* they do their jobs, but about *how much of themselves* managers devote to the job out of the total resources of capability available to them.

"We want your honest evaluation of how much of himself each of your subordinates expends in doing his job *relative to others around him at his level* of the organization."

major factors in the theory associated with the model. Therefore, gathering data from managers operating in distinctly different "reward climates" should result in more definite confirmation or disproof of the model. By knowing in advance the reward policies in these organizations, it should be possible to predict, on the basis of the model, many of the attitudes of the members. The failure of these predictions to be confirmed would, of course, lead to disconfirmation of parts of the model.

One other obvious need in connection with samples of respondents would involve comparing results for managers with those for nonmanagement rank-and-file personnel. In the discussion section of Chapter 6, considerable attention was devoted to the question of whether the positive and significant reward-fulfillment relationships with performance that we obtained from our sample were due primarily to the fact that the respondents worked in the management parts of organizations. Our speculations in that chapter could be tested rather easily by obtaining for rank-and-file workers data of the type obtained in the present study. One of the best ways to learn more about a particular subject population is to compare it with some other population. Hence, explicit management-nonmanagement comparisons could prove to be extremely valuable even where the ultimate interest is primarily in understanding managers and management.

From all that we have said in this chapter, it is obvious that future research in connection with refining and improving the theoretical model is both possible and necessary. It is our feeling, however, that the model in its present form can serve a useful function for the researcher by providing clues about the kinds of information that are needed to gain a greater comprehension of attitude-performance relationships in organizational settings.

CHAPTER 9

Some Implications for Practice

The model developed in this book, including the related empirical data, was constructed primarily for the purpose of gaining greater insight into a basic psychological problem connected with human behavior in organizations. Although the formulation of prescriptions for organizational practice was not the major stimulus for the attempt to design and test the model, some potential implications for practice do flow from it. In this final chapter, we shall discuss those features of the model and the empirical findings that seem to us to have relevance for organizational applications.

Four major areas of practical considerations are indicated by the conceptual model and the data. These are: an emphasis on determining reward values and perceived effort-reward probabilities; the importance of assessing role perceptions; the potential consequence of tying rewards more directly to differences in performance; and the benefits of continuous monitoring of employee attitudes and beliefs. In the pages that follow we shall take up each of these points in turn, and then conclude with a summary of our recommendations for organizations to consider in applying these ideas.

DETERMINING REWARD VALUES AND EFFORT–REWARD PROBABILITIES

At the beginning of the book, in Chapter 1, we stressed the point that a major portion of our model was based on contemporary approaches to motivation theory that are built around the concepts of valence and expectancy. In the present study, data were collected that were pertinent to both of these types of variables. On the basis of the conceptual model and the data (which were generally consistent with this particular part of the model), we feel justified in emphasizing to organizations the importance of these two sets of variables and the desirability of obtaining data relevant to them. Perhaps the primary advantage of collecting such data is that the information thus obtained would aid the organization in assessing the motivation of its employees to perform effectively in the future, since the model stresses that these types of attitudes are crucial in determining the effort that individuals expend in performing their job activities.

It is probably safe to say that many organizations do not, in fact, really know what their managers want from their jobs (i.e., value of rewards, in our model), and particularly they probably do not know what their managers see as the probabilities of obtaining these rewards in relation to the amount of effort they put forth in their jobs. If firms actually collected, especially on a regular basis, the kind of information we are describing, it could be a revealing experience. If there turned out to be considerable discrepancies between how top executives thought middle- and lower-level managers felt about reward values and effort-reward probabilities, and how these managers actually felt, this would not necessarily mean that a company should rush out and change its policies. It would indicate, however, that top echelon executives should carefully consider whether their current policies were, on the one hand, correct but not being communicated accurately and effectively to lower levels, or, on the other hand, whether the policies were in need of reformulation.

At the very least, obtaining systematic information on managers' reward desires, and their perceptions about rewards being based on effort, would constitute an essential first step in gaining the maximum motivational effects from the incentives the organization has at its disposal. And, except for the relatively small expenses involved in gathering this information, the more effective use of current rewards would cost the organization practically nothing. Furthermore, from the individual's standpoint, the organization's attempt to obtain such information should not smack of manipulation, since subsequent changes presumably would be based upon the knowledge and views of those affected. If, when organizations collect such data, they find that their managers have "incorrect" path-goal (effort-reward) expectations that need to be changed (from the organization's viewpoint), then straightforward and open discussion of the discrepancies in views could be extremely healthy for both the individual managers and the firm. We would argue that obtaining such information is at least as legitimate and valuable as obtaining traditional job satisfaction data.

ASSESSING ROLE PERCEPTIONS

The second area of practical implications for action based on the model concerns role perceptions. Our data strongly indicate that even when a manager exerts high effort in his job, the resulting performance may be relatively mediocre if his role perceptions are inaccurate. The moral here is that organizations need to consider paying more attention than they have in the past to assessing whether the individual correctly understands *where* his effort should be applied.

Companies devote a great deal of attention to attempting to increase the amount of effort that employees exert in their jobs, but often give considerably less attention (especially in management) to the question of the *direction* of such effort. (We are here speaking primarily of the more psychological aspects of the job, rather than the formal, technical duties of the job.) Our findings would imply that organizations might be able to improve the overall performance of their managers, without any corresponding increase in the amount of effort required of them, simply by focusing greater attention on role perceptions. Such attention, incidentally, does not mean that problems of undesired conformity would be increased for the individual manager. Quite the contrary would seem to be indicated. The more information that both the manager and the organization have about each other's role expectations, the more rational should be the decisions about whether a particular individual is employed in the right job and in the right organization. If it becomes clear to the individual that the organization wants or expects certain kinds of behavior in a particular job that he does not feel he could or should carry out, then he has a sounder basis for deciding to change organizations, or, at least, jobs within the same organization. Likewise, the organization has a more informed basis for making promotion, transfer, or separation decisions with regard to the individual manager.

ATTACHING REWARDS TO PERFORMANCE

The third, and perhaps most important, area of practical implications flowing from our model and related findings concerns the question of how closely organizations attach rewards to job performance. On paper, at least, most business organizations would probably claim that they reward their managers on the basis of merit. "Merit" is, in today's world, a very socially acceptable term, and ever since the rise of the professional manager in American business, the idea of rewarding managers on the basis of merit has become the socially accepted thing to do. However, in practice, as we pointed out in Chapter 4, even casual observation leads to the conclusion that in many firms this precept is honored by its violations. Managers in a wide variety of types of organizations are quick to tell an outsider that, while merit is not ignored in their companies, when the time comes for promotions or pay raises, other factors such as seniority, relationships with a particular superior, or just plain "fate" (i.e., being in the right place at the right time by chance) have a lot to do with how and when an individual gets rewarded. In other words, in many companies the connection between performance and rewards is at best a weak or hazy link. To elaborate on this point in more detail, let us consider some of our findings concerned with the relationships between attitudes toward pay and performance.

Two of the items in our questionnaires that were used to measure the degree to which pay is seen as a satisfier dealt with the psychological significance of raises. Answers to the items indicated that when raises are viewed as signifying progress in work or as rewards for good performance, pay is seen as a satisfier of a number of needs. Since other results of the present study indicate that the more pay is seen to depend on performance factors, the more motivated managers will be to perform their jobs effectively, it would seem that organizations should be quite concerned with the psychological impact of the raises they give. Companies that are content to give raises that are not seen as a form of recognition or reward may be missing a potent motivational inducement for better job performance as well as a chance to satisfy some of their managers' more important needs.

Too often organizations fall into one of the following traps that cause raises to lack incentive value: they either give across-the-board cost-of-living raises that have no incentive value; or they give recognition raises and then keep the information about them so secret that even the managers who receive them do not know how to evaluate them. The result of both these practices is that when a manager receives a raise, it does not provide the motivational boost that might come about if he received the same size raise under psychologically more meaningful conditions. The answer would appear to be for organizations not only to give raises that are based upon individual growth and merit, but also to give managers adequate feedback about raises so that each individual can evaluate the significance of his raise. One clue as to the type of pay policies that lead to pay raises being seen as recognition for good performance can be found in the large differences that appeared in our study between the government and private samples. As would be expected, the civil service policies of the government organizations apparently contribute to pay raises being seen as much less related to performance in that sample than in the private sample.[1] One implication of this finding is that organizations can foster the perception that pay raises are related to performance by appropriate pay programs.

One other implication in the area of pay policies concerns the relation of pay increases to opportunities to increase higher-order need satisfactions. A psychologically meaningful pay policy might be a method of satisfying these needs through good job performance. Raises keyed to performance growth seem to fit perfectly McGregor's (1960) criterion for healthy motivation, since they can satisfy the individual's needs while he is satisfying the organi-

---

[1]Appendix VI contains the data relevant to this point.

zation's needs by performing effectively. Thus, it may even be possible partially to satisfy and motivate "self-actualizing man" with economic rewards.

Of course, pay is not the only reward available in business organizations, although it is one of the most pervasive. Other rewards range all the way from those satisfying relatively lower-order needs, such as increased job security, to those satisfying higher-order needs, such as opportunities to take on more challenging tasks that facilitate individual development and growth. Here again, as with pay, organizations frequently are remiss in failing to establish a strong connection with differences in performance. Available evidence (e.g., Porter, 1964; Haire, Ghiselli, and Porter, 1966) indicates that managers, whether in this country or abroad, have extremely strong desires to satisfy higher-order needs but concurrently feel a deprivation of these needs in the typical organizational setting. The implication from these results is that organizations apparently have considerable opportunities to gain motivational leverage by increased attempts to attach appropriate rewards in the higher-order need areas of autonomy and self-actualization to differences in performance. It is a type of motivational impact that many organizations have failed to develop to the fullest. It is also an area in which individual managers could gain increased personal satisfaction while at the same time making greater contributions to organizational activities.

One other aspect of our findings that is relevant to the topic of attaching rewards to performance are the results from Chapter 6 dealing with the relationships between performance, on the one hand, and perceptions of fulfillment and satisfaction on the other hand. As brought out in that chapter, we did find that better performers reported significantly greater fulfillment and satisfaction. Nevertheless, the association fell far short of what potentially is possible. The reasons could be several, including errors of measurement in the performance ratings and the attitude instrument. Our hypothesis, however, is that a major factor preventing stronger performance-satisfaction relationships in our sample involved the reward practices—as distinguished from the reward policies—of the organizations studied.

In effect, we are making the following argument: in our investigation and in other studies of the performance-satisfaction relationship, the correlation between these two variables can be used as a diagnostic sign to indicate the effectiveness of "rewarding merit" policies. Most studies prior to our own have reported even weaker performance-satisfaction associations than we obtained. Our interpretation of those results is that many of them reflect the failure in practice to link differential rewards closely to differences in performance. Most of these studies, as we have noted, were carried out on rank-and-file workers, where the organization generally faces greater difficulties in implementing a merit reward policy.

It is our contention that if organizations are to improve their practices in rewarding merit to an extent that levels of satisfaction are closely related to levels of performance, three things must happen:

First, the rewards that are dispensed must be tailored to the needs and desires of the individual in terms of what *he* wants from performing his job effectively. In brief, the rewards need to be rewarding. To do this, organizations need to find out what job-related rewards are desired and what the individual currently sees as the consequences (both positive and negative) of putting forth a high level of effort in his job.

Second, superior performers need to be given more extrinsic rewards—and provided with more opportunities to gain intrinsic rewards—than inferior performers. This means the organization must be able to discriminate between good and poor performance in all jobs, must have the resources available to provide the necessary rewards, and must be willing to follow through and dispense them. The process can break down at any of these points. For example, methods to discriminate good from poor performance are often hastily devised and executed. Even where this is not the case, supervisors frequently feel that they cannot proceed to give the better performers the increased rewards they believe these individuals deserve. Sometimes, as in the case of pay, the "situation" simply will not allow it. At other times, however, the inability may be due to a lack of imagination on the part of the supervisor in devising appropriately rewarding opportunities. Finally, rewards are sometimes not given because the superior is unwilling to single out certain individuals for more rewards. Reasons for this can range all the way from the possible insecurity of the boss to the anticipated negative reactions of those not so rewarded.

Third, members of the organization need to see and believe that high levels of performance do lead to high levels of rewards. This involves making the reward process credible. We have already mentioned earlier in this chapter that the policy of pay secrecy can have the effect of disguising the fact that the best performers are getting the greatest monetary compensation. Whatever else it may result in, secrecy surrounding pay tends to reduce beliefs that amount of pay is based largely on quality of performance. Another factor that may reduce both credibility in, and trust of, the reward process concerns the basis of performance evaluations. If an individual in the organization feels that other people—e.g., his peers—are in as good a position as his boss to evaluate his work or better able to do so, a performance evaluation system that utilizes only the boss's ratings will be open to question. It would be our suggestion that companies consider, at least for some jobs and in some parts of the organization, supplementing ratings by superiors with those by peers, and perhaps even by the individual himself. While there are some obvious problems in this broadened base of performance evaluation, its possible strengthening of belief in the "rewarding of merit" process may indicate that its adoption would be a net gain for the organization (to say nothing of its possible positive consequences for the individual).

To sum up this section, we have suggested that the strength of the performance-satisfaction relationship may serve as a useful indicator of how well reward policies based on merit are working out in practice. If the relationship is low, we are suggesting that organizations examine their reward practices to see if the most appropriate (from the point of view of the receiver) rewards are being provided, if better performers are in fact given more rewards —or at least more opportunities to get them—than less adequate performers, and if the policy of rewarding merit is perceived as such by members of the organization.

CONTINUOUS MONITORING OF JOB ATTITUDES

The fourth and final area of practical implications does not flow directly from the model, but is consistent with it and with the various points we have previously discussed. We are referring to the desirability, in terms of providing relevant practical information for the organization, of continuously monitoring the job attitudes of employees. There are two aspects of continuous monitoring that deserve consideration: one pertains to new employees, and the other is concerned with gauging the impact of various changes in company policies and practices for employees who have been on the job and in the organization for a reasonable period of time.

With respect to new employees, we feel that both researchers and organizations have failed to pay sufficient attention to the possible rapid fluctuations in these employees' attitudes toward their job and the organization. Any adult, when confronted with a novel social situation, will expend considerable effort to try to organize his environment so that he can cope with it. During his early days in a new situation his views of the environment are quite likely to undergo fairly frequent, and perhaps large, changes. If the attitude progress of each new employee were followed, say, daily for the first several weeks on the job, it might be possible to spot "trouble" (in terms of short-term turnover) while there was still time to prevent it.

This daily attitude appraisal approach for new employees is predicated on two well documented facts: that turnover is most likely to occur during the employee's first month on the job, and that satisfaction levels are related to amount of turnover. Specifically, we are suggesting that organizations consider having newly-hired workers fill out very brief (i.e., taking less than a minute to fill out) questionnaires at the end of each day for the first few weeks on a job, and then maybe each week for the next couple of months. The instrument, with several multiple-choice type check-off questions, could elicit opinions as to whether a day's experiences with the job, fellow workers, and the supervisor had lived up to expectations and whether, therefore, the employee felt satisfied. If appropriate procedures were instituted so that the new hire felt that he could be completely open and candid in answering the daily questionnaire, it would be relatively easy to plot the trend of his satisfaction level. If nothing else, this procedure might provide the new employee with a definite opportunity to discuss his feelings and uncertainties with a (hopefully) sympathetic listener. The exact mechanics of such an approach with recently hired individuals would have to be worked out for particular organizations and situations, but we feel that it is an idea that has not been sufficiently explored in the past. Not only are there possible practical benefits that might be gained, but also there are research possibilities that could be developed with this type of repetitive attitude assessment.

The other type of continuous monitoring of attitudes that we wish to discuss concerns using attitude measurements to determine the effect of various changes in organizational reward policies and practices. Earlier in this chapter we stressed that more attention needs to be given to studying the beliefs that employees have about the probabilities that rewards are based on effort. Such perceptions can, of course, be studied at any given point in time, but the most interesting measurements would be those taken at regular intervals over a period of time. This would lead us away from a static approach to the utilization of attitude data, and would allow us to see whether certain actions by the organization seem to result in the desired effects.

This type of continuous monitoring would involve time intervals of reasonable length. Since we are talking about measuring the attitudes of individuals who have been on the job for, say, at least six months, it means that the job attitude assessments should not be more often than every six or nine months. Enough time would have to elapse between measurements in order for the process not to become a nuisance to the individual and for there to be time enough for possible changes in the environment to occur. The chief objective in this type of continuous monitoring would be to tie attitude changes to specific changes in the environment. In this way, the organization could obtain systematic feedback on how its actions, particularly with respect to rewards and motivation, were being received.

Although this type of regular monitoring of attitudes may seem like an obviously sensible thing to do, we know of very few companies (though there are some notable exceptions) that carry this out systematically. Often, firms measure employee attitudes sporadically or only when trouble (often involving union relations) seems to be brewing. When data of this type are obtained, they frequently are difficult or impossible to interpret because comparable questions have not been asked in the near past. Even where organizations do collect attitude data on a more or less regular basis, the content of the questions seldom gets at the type of information—such as perceived effort-reward probabilities—that could be most useful in the long run. Thus, we are advocating combining the idea of continuous monitoring with the idea of focusing on reward values, effort-reward probabilities, and role perceptions.

SUMMARY RECOMMENDATIONS

As we noted at the beginning of this chapter, the development of prescriptions for organizational practices was not the primary aim of either the theoretical conceptions or the collection of the empirical data that have been described in this book. Nevertheless, we have felt a necessity to try to see where our ideas would lead if they were utilized for practical purposes. In this final section, we shall sum up our thinking along these lines. The spirit in which these proposals are offered is one of suggestions for organizations to consider.

1. Organizations should endeavor to measure certain types of attitudes or beliefs that go beyond the traditional (and still important) "satisfaction" attitudes. Specifically, they should measure:

   a) The values—both positive and negative—of possible rewards and consequences that could result from an individual's attempt to exert high levels of effort in his job.

   b) Perceptions of the probabilities that positively valued rewards can be obtained by applying high levels of effort; and, perceptions of the probabilities that negatively valued consequences will result from applying high levels of effort.

   c) Role perceptions—perceptions by organizational members concerning *where* they should be applying their efforts in their jobs.

2. Organizations should continue to obtain job satisfaction data, but should concentrate on determining how closely levels of satisfaction are related to levels of performance. Measures of such performance-satisfaction relationships can then be used as one type of diagnostic sign indicating how effectively reward policies are working out in practice.

3. Organizations should examine the operation of their reward

practices to determine if (a) they are working as planned, and (b) if they can be made more effective from a motivational point of view. One example would be to evaluate the positive and negative consequences to the organization, and to individual members, of relaxing secrecy restrictions surrounding the disbursement of compensation.

4. Organizations should consider adopting the practice of monitoring employee attitudes on a continuing basis. For new employees, this would mean brief measurements separated by relatively short intervals. For all other employees, it would mean measuring at longer but consistent intervals, and concentrating on various types of attitude content (as outlined in proposal #1 above) as well as on the regularity of the process.

The above proposals will not guarantee any immediate improvements in individual or organizational performance. However, their adoption may serve to broaden the bases of decision making with respect to personnel policies and practices within the organization.

The Pay Questionnaire

[Introductory Instructions][1]

This questionnaire is part of a research study of management positions and jobs. The aim of this part of the study is to find out how individuals in management look at the pay for their positions.

By the term "pay" we mean the total income you receive from your position with the company—including both basic salary and whatever fringe benefits and special incentive income you may receive.

This is *not* a study of individual persons or of individual companies, but of managers as a professional group. The questionnaire is numbered so that respondents can be placed in the organization structure and in order that a follow-up letter can be sent to those individuals who fail to respond initially.

On the following pages you will find several different kinds of questions. Specific instructions will be given at the beginning of each part of the questionnaire.

There are no "trick" questions. All that we ask is that you try to answer as honestly and candidly as possible. Under no circumstances will your individual responses be made available to anyone

---

[1]Titles of the parts of the questionnaires and forms (bracketed headings) in Appendixes I–IV were not in the actual questionnaires and forms distributed to the respondents and raters. These titles are included here to help the reader identify the different parts of each instrument.

in your organization. Your completed questionnaire should be mailed directly to the University in the envelope enclosed.

In advance, we wish to thank you for your participation in this study. It is through management's cooperation in studies such as this that we all advance our understanding of the process of management.

[How Pay Is Determined]

In the section below, you will see several characteristics or qualities that are often used to determine individuals' pay. Please indicate how important your organization considers these for determining *your* present pay. This can be done by using the seven-point scale below each characteristic, which looks like this:

(unimportant)   1   2   3   4   5   6   7   (important)

You are to circle the number on the scale that represents the importance of the characteristic being rated. Low numbers represent low or unimportant characteristics. If you think your organization considers a given characteristic as unimportant in determining the pay for your management position, you would circle numeral 1. If you think it is "just a little" important you would circle numeral 2, and so on. For each scale circle only one number.

Please do not omit any scales.

1. Length of your service in the organization.
   (unimportant)   1   2   3   4   5   6   7   (important)
2. Your education, training and experience.
   (unimportant)   1   2   3   4   5   6   7   (important)
3. Your administrative skill.
   (unimportant)   1   2   3   4   5   6   7   (important)
4. Amount of responsibility and pressure in your job.
   (unimportant)   1   2   3   4   5   6   7   (important)
5. Quality of your job performance.
   (unimportant)   1   2   3   4   5   6   7   (important)
6. Your productivity on the job.
   (unimportant)   1   2   3   4   5   6   7   (important)
7. Amount of effort you expend on the job.
   (unimportant)   1   2   3   4   5   6   7   (important)

8. Scarcity of your skills in the labor market.

   (unimportant)   1   2   3   4   5   6   7   (important)

9. Your contribution to the technical and scientific knowledge of your organization.

   (unimportant)   1   2   3   4   5   6   7   (important)

[Satisfaction with Pay]

In the section below are listed several characteristics connected with the pay for your management position. For each such characteristic you will be asked to give three ratings.

   a) How much of the characteristic is there now?

   b) How much of the characteristic do you think there should be?

   c) How important is this characteristic to you?

Each rating will be on a seven-point scale which will look like this:

   (minimum)   1   2   3   4   5   6   7   (maximum)

You are to circle the number on the scale that represents the amount of the characteristic being rated. Low numbers represent low or minimum amounts and high numbers high or maximum amounts. If you think there is very little of the characteristic, you would circle the numeral 1. If you think there is a little bit, you would circle numeral 2, and so on. If you think there is a great deal but not a maximum amount, you would circle numeral 6. For each scale, circle only one number.

Please do not omit any scales.

1. The pay for my management position:

   a) How much is there now? (min)   1 2 3 4 5 6 7   (max)

   b) How much should there be?   1 2 3 4 5 6 7

   c) How important is this to me?   1 2 3 4 5 6 7

[NOTE: Three other characteristics contained in the actual questionnaire are omitted here because they are not relevant to the measure of satisfaction with pay.]

[Pay as a Satisfier]

In the section below you will see a series of statements designed to measure your attitude about the pay you receive for your present job. Please indicate your agreement or disagreement. Use the scale below each statement.

For example: It is easier to work in cool weather than in hot.

                  X

: _____ : _____ : _____ : _____ : _____ :

    Strongly   Agree   Undecided   Disagree   Strongly
     Agree   Disagree

If you think it is easier to work in cool weather, put an X above "agree"; if you think it is much easier to work in cool weather, put a mark above "strongly agree." If you think it doesn't matter, put a mark above "undecided," and so on. Put your mark in a space, not on the boundaries.

There are no right or wrong answers. We are interested in your opinion about the statements which follow.

2. For me, raises have meant that I was progressing in my work.

: _____ : _____ : _____ : _____ : _____ :

    Strongly   Agree   Undecided   Disagree   Strongly
     Agree   Disagree

4. The raises I have received were rewards for good performance.

: _____ : _____ : _____ : _____ : _____ :

    Strongly   Agree   Undecided   Disagree   Strongly
     Agree   Disagree

6. In my job, pay is a form of recognition for a job well done.

: _____ : _____ : _____ : _____ : _____ :

    Strongly   Agree   Undecided   Disagree   Strongly
     Agree   Disagree

[NOTE: Other statements contained in the actual questionnaire are omitted here because they are not relevant to the measure of pay as a satisfier.]

[Demographic Data]

NOTE: TO HELP US IN THE STATISTICAL ANALYSIS OF THE DATA, WE NEED THE FOLLOWING INFORMATION:

1. Approximately what is your yearly salary from your position before taxes and other deductions? _____

2. Line or Staff (Check one) :
     _____ Staff Management
     _____ Line Management
     _____ Combined Line and Staff

3. Time in Present Position (Check one) :

_____ 0–½ yr.	_____ 4–5 yrs.
_____ ½–1 yr.	_____ 5–10 yrs.
_____ 1–2 yrs.	_____ 10–15 yrs.
_____ 2–3 yrs.	_____ More than 15 yrs.
_____ 3–4 yrs.	

4. Total Time with Organization (Check one) :

_____ 0–1 yr.	_____ 6–10 yrs.
_____ 1–2 yrs.	_____ 11–20 yrs.
_____ 3–5 yrs.	_____ Over 20 yrs.

5. Age (Check one) :

_____ 20–24	_____ 40–49
_____ 25–29	_____ 50–59
_____ 30–34	_____ 60 or over
_____ 35–39	

6. Education (Check one) :

_____ Some High School	_____ College Degree
_____ H.S. Diploma	_____ Some Graduate Work
_____ Some College	_____ Master's Degree
_____ Business College	_____ Ph.D. Degree

APPENDIX II

The Need Satisfaction and Role

Perception Questionnaire

[Need Satisfactions]

On the following pages will be listed several characteristics or qualities connected with your own management position. For each such characteristic, you will be asked to give three ratings.

a) How much of the characteristic is there now connected with your management position?

b) How much of the characteristic do you think should be connected with your management position?

c) How important is this position characteristic to you?

Each rating will be on a seven-point scale, which will look like this:

(minimum)   1   2   3   4   5   6   7   (maximum)

You are to circle the number on the scale that represents the amount of the characteristic being rated. Low numbers represent low or minimum amounts, and high numbers represent high or maximum amounts. If you think there is "very little" or "none" of the characteristic presently associated with the position, you would circle numeral 1. If you think there is "just a little," you would circle numeral 2, and so on. If you think there is a "great deal but not a maximum amount," you would circle numeral 6. For each scale, circle only one number.

Please do not omit any scales.

1. The feeling of self-esteem a person gets from being in my management position:
   a) How much is there now?   (min) 1 2 3 4 5 6 7 (max)
   b) How much should there be?   1 2 3 4 5 6 7
   c) How important is this to me?   1 2 3 4 5 6 7

2. The authority connected with my management position:
   a) How much is there now?   (min) 1 2 3 4 5 6 7 (max)
   b) How much should there be?   1 2 3 4 5 6 7
   c) How important is this to me?   1 2 3 4 5 6 7

3. The opportunity for personal growth and development in my management position:
   a) How much is there now?   (min) 1 2 3 4 5 6 7 (max)
   b) How much should there be?   1 2 3 4 5 6 7
   c) How important is this to me?   1 2 3 4 5 6 7

4. The prestige of my management position inside the company (that is, the regard received from others in the company):
   a) How much is there now?   (min) 1 2 3 4 5 6 7 (max)
   b) How much should there be?   1 2 3 4 5 6 7
   c) How important is this to me?   1 2 3 4 5 6 7

5. The opportunity for independent thought and action in my management position:
   a) How much is there now?   (min) 1 2 3 4 5 6 7 (max)
   b) How much should there be?   1 2 3 4 5 6 7
   c) How important is this to me?   1 2 3 4 5 6 7

6. The feeling of security in my management position:
   a) How much is there now?   (min) 1 2 3 4 5 6 7 (max)
   b) How much should there be?   1 2 3 4 5 6 7
   c) How important is this to me?   1 2 3 4 5 6 7

7. The feeling of self-fulfillment a person gets from being in my management position (that is, the feeling of being able to use one's own unique capabilities, realizing one's potentialities):
   a) How much is there now?   (min) 1 2 3 4 5 6 7 (max)
   b) How much should there be?   1 2 3 4 5 6 7
   c) How important is this to me?   1 2 3 4 5 6 7

8. The prestige of my management position outside the company (that is, the regard received from others not in the company):
   a) How much is there now?   (min) 1 2 3 4 5 6 7 (max)
   b) How much should there be?   1 2 3 4 5 6 7
   c) How important is this to me?   1 2 3 4 5 6 7

9. The feeling of worthwhile accomplishment in my management position:
   a) How much is there now?   (min) 1 2 3 4 5 6 7 (max)
   b) How much should there be?   1 2 3 4 5 6 7
   c) How important is this to me?   1 2 3 4 5 6 7

10. The opportunity, in my management position, to give help to other people:
   a) How much is there now?   (min) 1 2 3 4 5 6 7 (max)
   b) How much should there be?   1 2 3 4 5 6 7
   c) How important is this to me?   1 2 3 4 5 6 7

11. The opportunity, in my management position, for participating in the setting of goals:
   a) How much is there now?   (min) 1 2 3 4 5 6 7 (max)
   b) How much should there be?   1 2 3 4 5 6 7
   c) How important is this to me?   1 2 3 4 5 6 7

12. The opportunity, in my management position, for participation in the determination of methods and procedures:
   a) How much is there now?   (min) 1 2 3 4 5 6 7 (max)
   b) How much should there be?   1 2 3 4 5 6 7
   c) How important is this to me?   1 2 3 4 5 6 7

13. The feeling of being informed in my management position:
   a) How much is there now?   (min) 1 2 3 4 5 6 7 (max)
   b) How much should there be?   1 2 3 4 5 6 7
   c) How important is this to me?   1 2 3 4 5 6 7

14. The opportunity to develop close friendships in my management position:
   a) How much is there now?   (min) 1 2 3 4 5 6 7 (max)
   b) How much should there be?   1 2 3 4 5 6 7
   c) How important is this to me?   1 2 3 4 5 6 7

15. The feeling of pressure in my management position:
   a) How much is there now?   (min) 1 2 3 4 5 6 7 (max)
   b) How much should there be?   1 2 3 4 5 6 7
   c) How important is this to me?   1 2 3 4 5 6 7

[Role Perceptions]

The purpose of this part of the questionnaire is to obtain a picture of the traits you believe are most necessary for success in YOUR PRESENT MANAGEMENT POSITION.

Below is a list of 12 traits arranged randomly. Rank these 12 traits from 1 to 12 in the order of their importance for success in your present management position.

For example, if you thought "Intelligent" was the most important trait for success in your present management position, you would put the number "1" in the space in front of "Intelligent." If you thought "Efficient" was the second most important trait, you would put the number "2" in front of "Efficient," and so on until the last space that is left would get the number "12," since it is the least important trait in your estimation.

IMPORTANT:

1. Number 1 stands for the *most* important, and 12 for the least important trait.

2. Be sure that *each* space is filled by a different number, corresponding to your rank of the trait.

Traits to be ranked (from 1 to 12)

_____ Efficient

_____ Forceful

_____ Cooperative

_____ Adaptable

Please check:

_____ Imaginative

_____ Independent

Have you used

_____ Cautious

all the numbers

_____ Intelligent

from 1 to 12?

_____ Self-confident

_____ Agreeable

_____ Decisive

_____ Tactful

APPENDIX III

Self-Rating Form

The purpose of this form is to determine how you rate yourself relative to others in your organization with similar management duties. You will be asked to rate yourself for characteristics on a seven-point scale which will look like this.

(low)   1   2   3   4   5   6   7   (high)

You are to circle the number on the scale that represents where you stand compared to others with similar management duties. If you think you are low on the characteristic, you would circle the numeral 1. If you think that you are a little less than average as compared with others with similar management duties, you would circle the numeral 3, and so on. For each scale, circle only one number.

Please do not omit any scales.

5. Quality of your job performance.
    (low)   1   2   3   4   5   6   7   (high)

6. Your productivity on the job.
    (low)   1   2   3   4   5   6   7   (high)

7. Amount of effort you expend on the job.
    (low)   1   2   3   4   5   6   7   (high)

[NOTE: Five other rating scales contained on the actual questionnaire are omitted here because they are not relevant to self-ratings of job performance.]

Superiors' Ranking Form

On each of the following pages you will find a different aspect of managerial job performance. You are to rank your subordinates on each of these aspects of job performance. You should assign a "1" to the subordinate who you feel stands highest on the factor considered. A "2" should be assigned to the subordinate who you feel stands second highest on the factor, and so on, until each subordinate listed receives a different number for his rank.

The data we are gathering will be used only as part of our research project on management job attitudes. The responses of individual managers will be held in the strictest confidence.

It is particularly important to the success of this project that you complete this form. Without the information from this form, data which are being gathered from your subordinates will be of no value.

Quality of Job Performance

It is well known that managers differ widely in their overall job performance. Below you will see the names of some of your subordinates. Would you please rank them on the basis of how well you feel they are performing their jobs?

REMEMBER:
1. Number *1* should be given to the subordinate who ranks highest on this factor.

2. Be sure that each subordinate is given a different number, corresponding to your rank of the subordinate.

RANK

[Names]

Effort Expended

The amount of effort a manager expends on the job is not always reflected in the quality of the manager's job performance. Thus, it is important to evaluate the amount of effort a manager expends on the job separately from the quality of his overall job performance. Would you please rank the following of your subordinates on the basis of how much effort you feel they expend on their jobs?

REMEMBER:

1. Number *1* should be given to the subordinate who ranks highest on this factor.
2. Be sure that each subordinate is given a different number, corresponding to your rank of the subordinate.

RANK

[Names]

[NOTE: Two other dimensions of managerial behavior to be ranked by superiors were contained on the original questionnaire but are omitted here because they are not relevant to job performance.]

APPENDIX V

Importance of Job Performance Factors

Mean Scores on the Importance Seen Attached
to Job Performance Factors by the Private Industry Sample and
by the Government Sample

Attitude Measures	Mean Private Industry Sample	Mean Government Sample	Differ- ence	t
Q5. Quality of Job Performance	5.59	4.55	1.04	8.00*
Q6. Productivity on the Job	5.42	4.15	1.27	9.77*
Q7. Effort Expended on the Job	4.85	3.80	1.05	7.29*
Index of Probability that Pay Depends upon Performance	15.87	12.76	3.11	7.59*

*$p < .01$

Degree to Which Pay Is Seen as a Satisfier

Means Scores on the Degree to Which Pay Is Seen as a Satisfier by
the Private Industry Sample and by the Government Sample

Attitude Measures	Mean Private Industry Sample	Mean Government Sample	Differ- ence	t
Q2. Raises Have Meant Progressing in Work 3.62		3.04	.58	6.24*
Q4. Raises Were Reward for Good Performance 3.41		2.84	.57	6.33*
Q6. Pay Is Recognition for Job Well Done 3.32		2.60	.72	8.18*
Index of Pay as a Satisfier 10.48		8.51	1.97	7.04*

*p < .01

Bibliography

ADAMS, J. S. Toward an understanding of inequity. *Journal of Abnormal and Social Psychology,* 1963, **67**, 422–36.

ADAMS, J. S. Injustice in social exchange. In L. Berkowitz (ed.), *Advances in experimental social psychology,* vol. 2. New York: Academic Press, 1965, 267–99.

ATKINSON, J. W. *An introduction to motivation.* Princeton, N.J.: Van Nostrand, 1964.

BAXTER, B. "Presidential address." Presented to Division 14, American Psychological Association, Chicago, 1965.

BRAYFIELD, A. H., AND CROCKETT, W. H. Employee attitudes and employee performance. *Psychological Bulletin,* 1955, **52**, 396–424.

BROWN, J. A. C. *The social psychology of industry.* Baltimore: Penguin, 1954.

BROWN, W. *Piecework abandoned.* London: Heineman, 1962.

CHALUPSKY, A. B. Incentive practices as viewed by scientists and managers of pharmaceutical laboratories. *Personnel Psychology,* 1964, **17**, 385–401.

COCH, L., AND FRENCH, J. R. P., JR. Overcoming resistance to change. *Human Relations,* 1948, **1**, 512–32.

DAVIDSON, D., SUPPES, P., AND SIEGEL, S. *Decision-making: An experimental approach.* Stanford, Calif.: Stanford University Press, 1957.

DUNNETTE, M. D., CAMPBELL, J. P., AND HAKEL, M. D. Factors contributing to job satisfaction and job dissatisfaction in six occupational groups. *Organizational Behavior and Human Performance,* 1967, **2**, 143–74.

EDWARDS, W. The theory of decision making. *Psychological Bulletin,* 1954, **51**, 380–417.

ENGLISH, E. B., AND ENGLISH, AVA C. *A comprehensive dictionary of psychological and psychoanalytical terms.* New York: Longmans, Green and Co., 1958.

ERAN, M. Relationship between self-perceived personality traits and job attitudes in middle management. *Journal of Applied Psychology,* 1966, **50**, 424–30.

FESTINGER, L. *A theory of cognitive dissonance.* Evanston, Ill.: Row, Peterson, 1957.

FLEISHMAN, E. A., AND PETERS, D. R. Interpersonal values, leadership attitudes, and "managerial success." *Personnel Psychology,* 1962, **15,** 127–44.

GALBRAITH, J. R. *Motivational determinants of job performance.* Unpublished Ph.D. dissertation, University of Indiana, 1966.

GEORGOPOULOS, B. S., MAHONEY, G. M., AND JONES, M. W., JR. A path-goal approach to productivity. *Journal of Applied Psychology,* 1957, **41,** 345–53.

GORDON, L. V. *Manual for administering the survey of interpersonal values.* Chicago: Science Research Associates, 1960.

GUION, R., AND GOTTIER, R. Validity of personality measures in personnel selection. *Personnel Psychology,* 1965, **18,** 135–64.

HAIRE, M., GHISELLI, E. E., AND PORTER, L. W. Psychological research on pay: An overview. *Industrial Relations,* 1963, **3,** 3–8.

HAIRE, M., GHISELLI, E. E., AND PORTER, L. W. *Managerial thinking: An international study.* New York: Wiley, 1966.

HAY, J. E. *The relationship of certain personality variables to managerial level and job performance among engineering managers.* Unpublished Ed.D. thesis, Temple University, 1964.

HAYS, W. L. *Statistics for psychologists.* New York: Holt, Rinehart & Winston, 1963.

HERZBERG, F., MAUSNER, B., PETERSON, R. O., AND CAPWELL, DORA F. *Job attitudes: Review of research and opinion.* Pittsburgh: Psychological Service of Pittsburgh, 1957.

HERZBERG, F., MAUSNER, B., AND SNYDERMAN, BARBARA. *The motivation to work,* 2d ed. New York: Wiley, 1959.

HOLLINGWORTH, H. L. *Judging human character.* New York: Appleton, 1922.

HULL, C. L. Special review: Thorndike's fundamentals of learning. *Psychological Bulletin,* 1935, **32,** 807–23.

HULL, C. L. *Principles of Behavior.* New York: Appleton-Century-Crofts, 1943.

HULL, C. L. *A behavior system.* New Haven, Conn., Yale University Press, 1952.

JONES, L. V., AND JEFFREY, T. E. A quantitative analysis of expressed preferences for compensation plans. *Journal of Applied Psychology,* 1964, **49,** 201–10.

JONES, M. R., ed. *Nebraska symposium on motivation.* Lincoln: Nebraska University Press, 1959, **7**.

KATZ, D., MACCOBY, N., AND MORSE, NANCY. *Productivity, supervision and morale in an office situation.* Ann Arbor, Mich., Institute for Social Research, 1950.

KATZ, D., MACCOBY, N., GURIN, G., AND FLOOR, L. G. *Productivity, supervision and morale among railroad workers.* Ann Arbor, Mich., Institute for Social Research, 1951.

KATZELL, R. A. Industrial psychology. *Annual Review of Psychology,* 1957, **8**, 237–68.

KORNHAUSER, A. W., AND SHARP, A. A. Employee attitudes: Suggestions from a study in a factory. *Personnel Journal,* 1932, **10**, 393–404.

KRECH, D., CRUTCHFIELD, R. S., AND BALLACHEY, E. L. *Individual in society.* New York: McGraw-Hill, 1962.

LAWLER, E. E. Managers' perceptions of their subordinates' pay and of their superiors' pay. *Personnel Psychology,* 1965, **18**, 413–22 (a).

LAWLER, E. E. Should managers' compensation be kept under wraps? *Personnel,* 1965, **42**, 17–20 (b).

LAWLER, E. E. Ability as a moderator of the relationship between job attitudes and job performance. *Personnel Psychology,* 1966, **19**, 153–64 (a).

LAWLER, E. E. The mythology of management compensation. *California Management Review,* 1966, **9**, 11–22 (b).

LAWLER, E. E. Secrecy about management compensation: Are there hidden costs? *Organizational Behavior and Human Performance,* 1967, **2**, 182–89 (a).

LAWLER, E. E. The multitrait-multirater approach to measuring managerial job performance. *Journal of Applied Psychology,* 1967, in press, (b).

LAWLER, E. E., AND PORTER, L. W. Perceptions regarding management compensation. *Industrial Relations,* 1963, **3**, 41–49.

LAWLER, E. E., AND PORTER, L. W. Antecedent attitudes of effective managerial performance. *Organizational Behavior and Human Performance,* 1967, **2**, 122–42 (a).

LAWLER, E. E., AND PORTER, L. W. Performance as a determinant of job satisfaction. *Industrial Relations,* 1967, in press, (b).

LEWIN, K. *The conceptual representation and the measurement of psychological forces.* Durham, N.C.: Duke University Press, 1938.

LEWIN, K., LIPPITT, R., AND WHITE, R. K. Patterns of aggressive behavior in experimentally created "social climates." *Journal of Social Psychology,* 1939, **10**, 271–99.

LIKERT, R. *New patterns of management.* New York: McGraw-Hill, 1961.

McGREGOR, D. *The human side of enterprise.* New York: McGraw-Hill, 1960.

MAHONEY, T. Compensation preferences of managers. *Industrial Relations,* 1964, **3**, 135–44.

MASLOW, A. H. A theory of human motivation. *Psychological Review,* 1943, **50**, 370–96.

MASLOW, A. H. *Motivation and personality.* New York: Harper, 1954.

MAYO, E. *The social problems of an industrial civilization.* Cambridge, Mass., Harvard University Press, 1945.

MILLER, E. L. Job satisfaction of national union officials. *Personnel Psychology,* 1966, **19**, 261–74.

MÜNSTERBERG, H. *Psychology and industrial efficiency.* Boston: Houghton-Mifflin, 1913.

MYERS, M. S. Who are your motivated workers? *Harvard Business Review,* 1964, **42** (1), 73–88.

NEALEY, S. Pay and benefit preference. *Industrial Relations,* 1963, **3**, 17–28.

OLMSTED, M. S. Character and social role. *American Journal of Sociology,* 1957, **63**, 49–57.

PEAK, HELEN. Attitude and motivation. In JONES, M. R. (ed.) *Nebraska symposium on motivation.* Lincoln: University of Nebraska Press, 1955, **3**, 149–88.

PORTER, L. W. A study of perceived need satisfactions in bottom and middle management jobs. *Journal of Applied Psychology,* 1961, **45**, 1–10.

PORTER, L. W. Job attitudes in management: I. Perceived deficiencies in need fulfillment as a function of job level. *Journal of Applied Psychology,* 1962, **46**, 375–84.

PORTER, L. W. Job attitudes in management: II. Perceived importance of needs as a function of job level. *Journal of Applied Psychology,* 1963, **47**, 141–48.

PORTER, L. W. *Organizational patterns of managerial job attitudes.* New York: American Foundation for Management Research, Inc., 1964.

PORTER, L. W., AND HENRY, MILDRED M. Job attitudes in management: V. Perceptions of the importance of certain personality traits as a function of job level. *Journal of Applied Psychology,* 1964, **48**, 31–36.

PORTER, L. W., AND LAWLER, E. E. Properties of organization structure in relation to job attitudes and job behavior. *Psychological Bulletin,* 1965, **64**, 23–51.

PORTER, L. W., AND MITCHELL, V. F. A comparative study of need satisfactions in military and business hierarchies. *Journal of Applied Psychology,* 1967, **51**, 139–44.

RIESMAN, D. *The lonely crowd.* New Haven, Conn., Yale University Press, 1950.

ROADMAN, H. E. An industrial use of peer ratings. *Journal of Applied Psychology,* 1964, **48**, 211–14.

ROETHLISBERGER, F. J., AND DICKSON, W. J. *Management and the worker.* Cambridge, Mass., Harvard University Press, 1939.

ROSEN, H., AND WEAVER, C. G. Motivation in management: A study of four management levels. *Journal of Applied Psychology,* 1960, **44**, 386–92.

SCHEIN, E. H. *Organizational Psychology.* Englewood Cliffs, N. J.: Prentice-Hall, 1965.

SCHWARTZ, M. M., JENUSAITIS, E., AND STARK, H. Motivational factors among supervisors in the utility industry. *Personnel Psychology,* 1963, **16**, 45–53.

SEASHORE, S. E. Field experiments with formal organizations. *Human Organization,* 1964, **23**, 164–70.

SPENCE, K. W. *Behavior theory and conditioning.* New Haven, Conn., Yale University Press, 1956.

TANNENBAUM, A. *Social psychology of the work organization.* Belmont, Calif.: Wadsworth, 1966.

TAYLOR, D. W. Decision making and problem solving. In J. G. MARCH (ed.), *Handbook of organizations.* Chicago: Rand McNally, 1965, 48–86.

THORNDIKE, E. L. *Animal intelligence.* New York: Macmillan, 1911.

TOLMAN, E. C. *Purposive behavior in animals and men.* New York: Century, 1932.

TRIANDIS, H. C. Categories of thought of managers, clerks and workers about jobs and people in industry. *Journal of Applied Psychology,* 1959, **43**, 338–44.

VEROFF, J., ATKINSON, J. W., FELD, SHEILA C., AND GURIN, G. The use of thematic apperception to assess motivation in a nationwide interview study. *Psychological Monographs,* 1960, **74**, Whole No. 499.

VROOM, V. H. *Work and motivation.* New York: Wiley, 1964.

VROOM, V. H. *Motivation in management.* New York: American Foundation for Management Research, Inc., 1965.

WEICK, K. E. Laboratory experimentation with organizations. In J. G. MARCH (ed.), *Handbook of organizations.* Chicago: Rand McNally, 1965, 194–260.

WERNIMONT, P. F. *Intrinsic and extrinsic factors in job satisfaction.* Unpublished Ph.D. dissertation. University of Minnesota, 1964.

WHITLOCK, G. H. *Performance evaluation through psychophysics.* Unpublished paper, University of Tennessee, 1965.

WHITLOCK, G. H. Application of the psychophysical law to performance evaluation. *Journal of Applied Psychology,* 1963, **1**, 15–23.

WHYTE, W. F. *Money and motivation: An analysis of incentives in industry.* New York: Harper, 1955.

WHYTE, W. H., JR. *The organization man.* New York: Simon and Schuster, 1956.

WOODWARD, JOAN. *Management and technology.* London: Her Majesty's Stationery Office, 1958.

Name Index

Subject Index

A

Abilities and traits, definition and explanation of, 22–24
Attitudes; *see* Job attitudes

D

Data analysis, description of methods of, 52–55
Drive theory
differences from expectancy theory, 10–12
discussion of, 8–12

E

Effort
definition and explanation of, 21–22
hypothesized relation to fulfillment, 129–30
tests of, 137–40
hypothesized relation to pay, 62–63, 66
tests of, 71–75, 80–84
hypothesized relation to performance, 32–33
measures of
need for improvement in, 170
questionnaire items for, 196
probability of leading to reward, 19–21
role perceptions and, 104, 109–14
Effort-reward probability
definition and explanation of, 19–21
hypothesized feedback relation from rewards, 38–39
hypothesized relation to value of rewards, 31–32
implications of practice in determining, · 173–75
Expectancy theory
differences from drive theory, 10–12
discussion of, 9–14
preference for, 12–14
Extrinsic rewards; *see* Rewards

F

Feedback relationships; *see* Theoretical model
Financial incentives; *see* Pay
Fulfillment
findings, implications of, 140–50
hypothesized relation to effort, 129–30
tests of, 137–40
hypothesized relation to performance, 124–27, 129–30
tests of, 132–40
measures of, 130–32
questionnaire items for, 190–92

H

Hawthorne studies, role of pay in, 57–59
Herzberg theory
attitudes toward pay, 64–66, 90–91, 152
relation between performance and attitudes, 6, 149

I

Incentives; *see* Pay; Rewards; *and* Value of rewards
Inner-directed behavior; *see* Role perceptions
Intrinsic rewards; *see* Rewards

J

Job attitudes; *see also* Methodology *and* Satisfaction
continuous monitoring, implications for practice of, 180–83
definition of, 2
history of research on, 4–7
measurement of, 44–45
relation to performance, 1, 3, 4–5
previous research on, 5, 121–24
theories of, 6–7
Job behavior; *see also* Performance
measurement of, 45–48
Job performance; *see* Performance
Job satisfaction; *see* Satisfaction

This book has been set in 11 and 10 point Baskerville, leaded 2 points. Chapter numbers are in 12 point News Gothic Bold; chapter titles are 24 point Baskerville. The size of the type page is 26 by 44 picas.